T0311812

Cambridge Elements ≡

Elements in Eighteenth-Century Connections
edited by
Eve Tavor Bannet
University of Oklahoma
Markman Ellis
Queen Mary University of London

EIGHTEENTH-CENTURY ILLUSTRATION AND LITERARY MATERIAL CULTURE

Richardson, Thomson, Defoe

Sandro Jung
Fudan University

CAMBRIDGE
UNIVERSITY PRESS

Shaftesbury Road, Cambridge CB2 8EA, United Kingdom

One Liberty Plaza, 20th Floor, New York, NY 10006, USA

477 Williamstown Road, Port Melbourne, VIC 3207, Australia

314–321, 3rd Floor, Plot 3, Splendor Forum, Jasola District Centre,
New Delhi – 110025, India

103 Penang Road, #05–06/07, Visioncrest Commercial, Singapore 238467

Cambridge University Press is part of Cambridge University Press & Assessment,
a department of the University of Cambridge.

We share the University's mission to contribute to society through the pursuit of
education, learning and research at the highest international levels of excellence.

www.cambridge.org
Information on this title: www.cambridge.org/9781108977937

DOI: 10.1017/9781108973557

When citing this work, please include a reference to the DOI 10.1017/9781108973557

First published 2023

A catalogue record for this publication is available from the British Library.

ISBN 978-1-108-97793-7 Paperback
ISSN 2632-5578 (online)
ISSN 2632-556X (print)

Eighteenth-Century Illustration and Literary Material Culture

Richardson, Thomson, Defoe

Elements in Eighteenth-Century Connections

DOI: 10.1017/9781108973557
First published online: May 2023

Sandro Jung
Fudan University

Author for correspondence: Sandro Jung, sjung@fudan.edu.cn

Abstract: This Element studies eighteenth- and early nineteenth-century instances of transmediation, concentrating on how the same illustrations were adapted for new media and how they generated novel media constellations and meanings for these images. Focusing on the 'content' of the illustrations and its adaptation within the framework of a new medium, case studies examine the use across different media of illustrations (comprehending both the designs for book illustrations and furniture prints) of three eighteenth-century works: Defoe's *Robinson Crusoe* (1719), Thomson's *The Seasons* (1730) and Richardson's *Pamela* (1740). These case studies reveal how visually enhanced material culture not only makes present the literary work, including its characters and story-world. But they also demonstrate how, through processes of transmediation, changes are introduced to the illustration that affect comprehension of that work. This title is also available as Open Access on Cambridge Core.

This Element also has a video abstract:
Cambridge.org/Eighteenth-Century Illustration and Literary Material Culture_Jung

Keywords: illustration, material culture, literary history, mediation, transmediality

ISBNs: 9781108977937 (PB), 9781108973557 (OC)
ISSNs: 2632-5578 (online), 2632-556X (print)

Contents

1 Transmediation, Illustration and Material Culture

Illustrations of literature often developed lives beyond the vision expressed in the artist's original book or print design, especially when they were adapted for use on other objects. In the process of moving from one object to another, these illustrations were made to function multi-medially. As such, they advanced visual interpretations of the works and characters they visualized, as part of a new medium. This process of illustrations moving from one object to another, a process here termed 'transmediation', is the subject of this Element. Transmediation defines how visual information and material properties of media cross-fertilized and generated new meanings. It is demarcated conceptually from the limiting new media and virtual reality contexts of 'remediation' in that the latter focuses on the replacement of a prior medium by a newer one, 'the representation of one medium in another' (Bolter and Grusin, 1999, p. 45). This new medium, according to Jay David Bolter and Richard Grusin, is characterized by 'transparent immediacy', the result of 'attempts to achieve immediacy by ignoring or denying the presence of the medium and the act of remediation' (1999, p. 46). Transmediation as a practice predating Bolter and Grusin's concept of remediation involves a process by which a media configuration consisting of material object and visual structure is altered; the signifier retained in the reconfiguration of literary 'content' is the illustration. It involves acts of medial transfer in the form of illustrations and of 'plots and characters that [can] appear in a variety of different media' (Straumann, 2015, p. 256). By contrast, remediation in this account of transmediation will be used in only one, more general sense defined by Bolter and Grusin: specifically, the 'repurposing' of a medial property and its 'reuse ... in another' medium (Bolter and Grusin, 1999, p. 45).

Two examples will demonstrate transmediation at work. Specifically, I will explore the mobility of the same illustrations across media as well as how, depending on the context of the object to which the illustration is transferred, new meanings are generated. The 1793 Perth edition of *The Seasons* contained a specially commissioned illustration by Charles Catton that introduced a scene of shipwreck and included five sailors during a storm (Figure 1). The meaning of the plate was relationally determined as part of the textual passage that was reproduced at the bottom of the engraving. This clear, interpretative relationship to Thomson's work, however, was complicated once the design was repurposed for use in James Ballantyne's 1810 edition of *Robinson Crusoe*. Neither Catton's intention to create a faithful representation of the scene from Thomson's 'Summer' nor the meaning that readers could establish as part of reading visualization and printed verse alongside one another informed the functioning of the illustration in Ballantyne's edition. Removed from the relational meaning-making of the 1793 edition, the same design in Ballantyne's

Figure 1 Copper-engraved book illustration of '[A Shipwreck]'
(15.8 × 21.4 cm), designed by Charles Catton and engraved by Francis
Chesham, *The Seasons* (Perth: R. Morison, 1793). Collection Sandro Jung.

volume signified differently (Figure 2). The original sailor standing and holding
on to a rope, who in Thomson's poem was nameless, is now transformed into the
title protagonist, Defoe's text being used to gloss that which is depicted by the
image.

Relational meaning-making involving the same reused designs that illustrate
different works demonstrates that the meaning of an illustration is contingent on
both the context in which it appears and the medium in and on which it is realized.
These context-defined meaning factors are especially relevant once different
material contexts of objects and their uses are considered. For example,
Angelica Kauffman's 1782 illustration of a moment in Thomson's tragic-
sentimental tale of Celadon and Amelia was produced as a stand-alone print.
Yet it was applied to other objects, including enamelled Duesbury vases, mourning pendants and love tokens. Since the objects possessed associated uses that
hinged on the occasion that defined their being given, the transmediation of the
illustration on the miniature pendants and love tokens resulted in diametrically
opposed contextual–relational meanings. Kauffman's image on the mourning
pendant modally and iconically invoked Amelia's death, anticipating the tragic
ending of Thomson's vignette, which is not visually depicted but hinted at

Figure 2 Redacted wood-engraved version of Catton's illustration
(5.5 × 8.3 cm), *The Life and Adventures of Robinson Crusoe*
(Edinburgh: Ballantyne, 1810). Collection Sandro Jung.

through the lightning (Figure 3). The love token, by contrast, highlights the deep
emotional connection between Celadon and Amelia (Figure 4). This gift for
a lover introduces the danger of the thunderstorm, centralizing the lovers as
a unit that is stable and will not be destroyed by the lightning. The transmedial
uses of Kauffman's (and Catton's) illustrations demonstrate changes in meaning,
including the modal and tonal revision and re-inscription of the designs that are
effected by both context and medium.

This Element will study eighteenth- and early nineteenth-century instances of
transmediation, concentrating on how the same illustrations were 'adapted
to . . . new media and their modes of mediation and representation of cognitive
import' (Domingos and Cardoso, 2021, p. 92). By focusing on the 'content' of
the illustrations and its adaptation within the framework of a new medium, case

Figure 3 Mourning pendant, with sepia painting of Celadon and Amelia
(7 × 4 cm), c. 1790. Collection Sandro Jung.

studies examine the use across different media of illustrations (comprehending
the designs for both book illustrations and furniture prints for framing) of three
eighteenth-century works: Daniel Defoe's *The Life and Strange Surprizing
Adventures of Robinson Crusoe* (1719), James Thomson's *The Seasons*
(1730) and Samuel Richardson's *Pamela: or, Virtue Rewarded* (1740). These
case studies will reveal that material culture incorporating illustrations forms
part of 'a *culture* based on the visual, on modalities of visualization, the
production and consumption of visual matter' (de Bolla, 2004, p. 4), which
conceived of literature as much as a textual as a visualizable, potentially
ekphrastic phenomenon.

The case study texts share an important characteristic: the episodic, narrative
character of both novels and the interpolated tales from Thomson's blank verse
poem. This character recommended the tragic-sentimental stories from *The
Seasons* to compilers of miscellanies and, in the case of Defoe and Richardson's

Figure 4 Love token, with enamel painting of Celadon and Amelia on ivory
(2 × 4 cm), c. 1790. Collection Sandro Jung.

novels, induced booksellers to issue chapbook epitomes that highlighted parts of
particular interest, including the protagonists' adventures, trials and dangers. These
textually embedded vignettes offered micro-stories that showcased characters
involved in actions and meaningful settings at the same time that they conveyed
particular sentiments and ideologies. They served as metonymic placeholders for
entire works, encompassing moments that helped readers to make sense of the
characters' role within a larger narrative; they also piqued 'interest', inducing
readers to (re)familiarize themselves with the work from which the vignettes had
been singled out through illustration. James Beattie held that vignettes 'animate'
literary works, for 'human actions are the columns and rafters [of "the poetical

fabric"], that give it stability and elevation' (Beattie, 1778, II, p. 30). These works' characters existed in the realm of 'the textual commons', essentially providing a shared imaginative property of the 'social canon'. Reconfiguration through different 'modes of iterability' fashioned by the makers of visual material culture reintroduced them to audiences who were supposed to recover and reimagine the stories of these media (Brewer, 2005, p. 78, p. 13). Their 'repetition through adaptation kept the … [stories of which these vignettes were a part] relevant and recognizable' (Lopez Szwydky, 2020, p. 101). Visual adaptation conjured story-worlds, transmediation repeatedly changing the dynamics and components of the stories; in the process, it invited audiences to reconstruct the authors' textual worlds and 'immerse' themselves in them (Wolf, 2012, p. 19). Even though the illustrations visualized scenes from works of different genres, genre and modal identities proved subservient to the vignettes' symbolic-narrative meanings highlighted in their visualization.

Offering an original perspective that brings together illustration studies, transmediation studies and material culture research, this Element focuses on what Thomas Bremer regards as essential in literary material culture: 'the interplay of materiality and text' (Bremer, 2020, p. 350). It examines the connections between illustrations and the physical objects that adapt them, including the processes of medial integration that obscure the illustrations' origin as distinct from these objects. The Element argues for the wide reach of literary illustrations as part of a hitherto largely uncharted material culture whose makers deploy the creative-transformational mechanisms of transmediation. Clearly, transmediation not only enriches the meaning of illustrations but also complicates meaning through the material and social practices related to the object incorporating the illustration. My examination concentrates on one of the two principal research areas of literary material culture: the study of how material culture harnesses iconic textual cultures to promote literariness. As such, it does not adopt the more established practice that investigates the presence of objects and material practices in literature.[1]

The Element will particularly focus on a discussion of ceramics, a medium (or substrate) that was especially versatile: depending on their particular 'primary intended use', ceramic objects could function variously (Brooks, 2010, p. 158). It will probe how producers of different objects recruiting the same

---

[1] The latter focus on the representation and use of material culture in literature has resulted in specialist studies such as, among others, Julie Park's 2010 book on the artificial life of objects, Chloe Wigston Smith's 2013 monograph on women, work and dress, and two themed issues on 'Material Fictions' of *Eighteenth-Century Fiction* (31:1 (2018) and 32:2 (2019)). Research in the former area is scant, although Angelika Müller-Scherf's 2009 account of the Meissen *Werther* porcelain demonstrates the use of book illustrations on porcelain, while not, however, exploring transmediation at work.

illustrations advanced particularized versions of iconically invoked works. Importantly, it will extend traditional foci in literary illustration studies by going beyond the ways in which text–image relationships are commonly explored within the paratextual framework of a codex or between a text and an extra-textual print. In doing so, I will explore the readability of material culture that mediates literary illustrations not as alien, iconotextual features but as 'naturalized', integral elements of the material constitution of objects that represent textual extensions and sites of literary reception (Mole, 2017, p. 2).

Studying the transmedial use of the same illustrations of literary works sets this Element apart from important scholarship on the illustrations of eighteenth-century literature: David Blewett on the illustrations of *Robinson Crusoe*, Robert Halsband on *The Rape of the Lock*, Tom Keymer and Peter Sabor, as well as Lynn Shepherd, on *Pamela*, Peter Wagner on *Gulliver's Travels* and William Blake Gerard and Mary-Céline Newbould on *Tristram Shandy* and *A Sentimental Journey*. These scholars' considerations of illustrations largely concentrate on illustrated editions, applying 'a resolute focus on word and image' (Ionescu, 2011, p. 29) within a codex-defined framework of meaning. As such, they restrict meaning and do not look to illustrated material culture. They contextualize illustrations as iconic devices, framed by the object of the 'bi-modal' (Ionescu, 2011, p. 8) – rather than the multi-modal and multi-medial – book. Paul Goldman reinforces this notion, observing that the 'central purpose of illustrations' is 'interpretation' (Goldman and Cooke, 2012, p. 15) of that which textually surrounds the illustration in the codex. His notion of the 'discipline' of illustration studies does not include transmedial uses but frequently conceives of illustrations as high-end visual culture reduced in size.[2] This understanding of the 'discipline', however, no longer holds, with recent interventions by Sandro Jung and David F. Taylor respectively challenging Goldman's conception of the field.

Jung embeds illustrations of *The Seasons* within a wider (printed) visual culture that includes more than merely paper-based objects (Jung 2015). As an exception in the field of illustration studies, he extends the study of diverse target audiences beyond Britain to transnational considerations of the visual reception of Thomson's poem and to the transformation of the same images across editions. By contrast, Taylor examines 'the process of narrativizing

---

[2] Most of the studies of eighteenth-century authors' illustrated works privilege upmarket editions and high-cultural paintings over those visualizations that were included in such cheap print media as chapbooks – even though the latter, including what Keymer and Sabor term 'the least distinguished of the later illustrated editions' of *Pamela* (Keymer and Sabor, 2005, p. 172), issued by Francis Newbery in 1769, would have reached many more readers than the illustrations they centralize in their account.

politics' (Taylor, 2018, p. 2) in satirical prints and their parody of literary works. He is concerned with how these prints responded to (performative) renderings of Shakespeare, Milton and Swift and how they catered to a politically aware elite. His focus is on parody rather than the re-creative, adaptive transmediation of existing book illustrations for ends that support the marketing of visually inscribed objects. Even though he does not study inter-iconic relationships between book illustrations and satirical prints, such prints reworking book illustrations did in fact exist: Thomas Rowlandson produced a series of prints, 'The Four Seasons of Love', which in a radical way transmediated a set of illustrations for *The Seasons* (Jung, 2020, pp. 301–8).

Because multiple modalities characterize the multi-medial literary culture to be investigated, it calls for a reconsideration of how illustrations are commonly understood by scholars of illustrated books. As indicated by the examples introduced at the beginning of this section, the transformative use of illustrations across media challenges widely held assumptions. Restricting consideration to the medial framework of intra-textual, edition-specific illustrations, on the one hand, and to the intermedial rapport between texts and separately issued prints or paintings, on the other, obscures the multi-medial – rather than bi-medial (or what Ionescu terms 'bi-modal') – functioning of illustrations (Peterssen, 2020, p. 273). According to Edward Hodnett, 'the primary function of the illustration of literature is to realize significant aspects of the text' (Hodnett, 1982, p. 13). But this understanding of the function of illustrations limits it to iconic paratext commissioned for works published in codex form and ignores illustrations harnessed by makers of literary material culture. For him, the value of illustration lies only in the fidelity and precision of the specific interpretive visualization of the typographical text it represents (Hodnett, 1982, p. 12). But the 'precise', exclusive text-specific image, as Hodnett comprehends it, does not reflect the evocative and allusive character of illustrations once transmediated and removed from the original words they previously visualized. Indeed, as I will argue, once embedded into a new medial context, they signify differently – representationally and symbolically – precisely because they form part of the social practices governing the use of the material culture of which they have become an integral part. Moreover, Hodnett's understanding of the function of illustration is limiting in its use of qualitative criteria that *may* apply to the text–image relationship within the codex. As Julia Thomas has noted, 'an illustration is not simply a "transposition" or "transformation" of the words, but stands in a nuanced relation of complementarity and conflict, sameness and difference' (Thomas, 2017, p. 3). It is Thomas's broadened notion of illustration that will inform my examinations of remediated visualizations of literature.

In order to make sense of the transmediation of illustrations, including how iconic, literary meaning is incorporated in a new, material medium, different kinds of literacy are required. Next to visual literacy (the ability to 'read' images at both representational and symbolic levels) and textual literacy (the ability to recognize motifs, scenes, intertextual connections between works or to recall allusions), those readers seeking to understand the entity of transmediated image and cultural object required material literacy. The latter concept encompasses not only the 'making practice, skill and knowledge' to produce goods but also, as Serena Dyer and Chloe Wigston Smith posit, those people not directly involved in the making of objects 'who mobilized their knowledge of making to comment upon, judge and inform their own activities as consumers and owners of material objects' (Dyer and Wigston Smith, 2020, p. 1). Different kinds of literacy frequently did not operate independently of one another but merged into what may be conceived of as a more comprehensive material–textual–symbolic literacy. This complex literacy, according to Caroline Winterer, enabled those eighteenth-century women drawing on the history of the classical past to harness this past for their own ends, as we can see when they copied illustrations and introduced them in such domestically produced material culture as embroidered textiles (Winterer, 2007, p. 30).

The examinations of the transmedial appropriation of illustrations in this Element build on recent work on the recycling of illustrations by different publishers (Jung, 2021), particularly since these illustrations are characterized by a mobility across media and geographical borders, which facilitated their meaningful recontextualization and altered meanings. They will conceive of illustrations as 'portal[s] between the text and its cultural context' (Haywood, Matthews and Shannon, 2019, p. 5), but also as part of 'the rambunctious materiality of eighteenth-century texts' (Barchas, 2003, p. 6), textuality being defined broadly to include material culture as long as it was 'produced with the intention of communicating a meaningful message that an audience could usually interpret' (Treharne and Willan, 2020, p. 2). Illustrations are 'gateways' to stories and the materiality of, and access to, the gateway, spatially constructed on the planar surface of a substrate, changes modally as the illustration is adapted. Transmedial adaptation involves 'a galvanizing force that drives storytelling' (Lopez Szwydky, 2020, p. 3) whereby the literary stories invoked iconically converge with those practices inherent in the making and social use of the material substrate. In the process, the stories conveyed by the image intersect with the cultural narrative, as part of which the objects adorned with the illustration operate; the two media cross-fertilize one another, the material agency of the object affecting the story-generative potential of the illustration. Rather than merely understanding this illustrative literary material culture in terms of epitexts that, according to Gérard Genette, exist in 'a virtually limitless physical and social space' (Genette, 1997, p. 344), the literary material culture discussed in this Element remains context-specific and catered to social practices that required their 'performance' to take place in delimited settings to fulfil their cultural function.

The increase of illustrations after the 1770s being reused on substrates other than paper was facilitated by technological innovation pertaining to the cost-effective reproduction of designs on materials ranging from voile fabric and silk to copper and ceramics. The hand-modelling and painterly application of pre-existing designs on literary material culture that had respectively characterized wax works and porcelain cups relating to the *Pamela* media event of the early 1740s were gradually replaced by transfer processes and transformed the industry. Even so, high-end productions such as unique porcelain objects still continued to be produced at the end of the century. By the 1820s, however, when illustrations from *Robinson Crusoe* were printed onto dessert plates, these wares had become mass-produced commodities. While the *Pamela* vogue had been defined by a small number of transmedially applied illustrations, the opposite proved to be the case in relation to *The Seasons*. The reason for the larger number was not purely technological but was grounded in the unprecedented number of illustrated editions of the poem that were published from the late 1770s onwards. Driven by the media interest surrounding the 1774 court decision in *Donaldson* v. *Becket* regarding the end of perpetual copyright, at the centre of which action had been the copyright of *The Seasons*, a new media event was triggered. It benefitted from the end of the copyright monopoly controlling the printing of editions of Thomson's poem and focused especially on Thomson's three most popular vignettes. As a result, an unprecedented transmedial visual culture developed in which illustrations from the large number of competing illustrated editions experienced new lives on non-book objects. The end of perpetual copyright also made possible the reprinting, in illustrated editions, of Defoe's novel – and to a lesser degree Richardson's by then less popular *Pamela* – by non-copyright-holding publishers. In one decade alone, the 1790s, illustrators produced a much larger number of visualizations of *Robinson Crusoe* than those that had appeared in the six decades following the work's original publication. These illustrations were part of a visual archive from which producers of literary material culture could choose freely those designs that suited the media products they manufactured.

The four sections that follow introduce detailed interpretive contextualizations of how artisans adapting existing designs for application to another medium intervened in the meaning-making process of the image: they created new meanings in relation to an inferred text or supported by a text gloss through visual revision of the illustration and its meaningful framing through the modal properties of the material substrate mediating the image. The material media introduced most often in the sections are ceramics of various kinds, ranging from high-end Derby porcelain, enamel miniatures and creamware, to porcelain figurines and French faience. This recurrence of the substrate is not coincidental and is related to the versatility and material properties of the ceramic medium to carry two-dimensional, planar illustrations or to realize these visualizations three-dimensionally. Ceramics repeatedly provided text–technological platforms for the display and embodiment of medially repurposed literary illustrations. Each section's object studies will demonstrate the adaptability of ceramics to be inscribed with literary–iconic meaning while, at the same time, also elucidating the particular interpretive relationships that these objects entertained with other textual media.

2 Re-signifying *Pamela*: From Snuff Box to Chapbook

Within months of the publication of Samuel Richardson's epistolary novel about a young servant girl's virtue being threatened by her would-be seducer's protestations of love and violence respectively, *Pamela, or Virtue Rewarded* (1740), not only 'help[ed] to inaugurate a shift in media practices' (Warner, 1998, p. 176), but it also, through the media event that it fed, metamorphosed from typographically fixed text and widely talked about narrative into a visual spectacle. In the process, 'the reader [was] . . . transformed into a spectator or beholder and the reading into a visual and aural event' (Chartier, 2007, p. 116). The media culture created by *Pamela* involved the production of a diverse visual and material culture: ranging from an illustrated fan and waxworks to illustrated editions and series of paintings; it visualized the trials of Richardson's protagonist, 'the merchandise at once appropriating and promoting his text' (Keymer and Sabor, 2005, p. 146). Pamela's trials in the household of her late benefactor's son and at his Lincolnshire estate, the testing of her virtue, her interactions with characters such as Mrs Jervis and Parson Williams and the predatory behaviour of Mr B and his housekeeper, Mrs Jewkes, offered a rich array of subjects that artists selected for iconic representation. Depending on the choice of episodes and on whether or not these artworks were authorially sanctioned, artists cast Pamela in a number of ways – from paragon of virtue to erotic figure.

The *Pamela* vogue was driven by the diversity of text-related objects produced, rather than their cross-referentiality and the production of media that incorporated earlier visualizations. The reuse of existing illustrations of the work would, of course, increase profit margins for manufacturers, but the avid demand for *Pamela*-related media products made specific differences in iconic realization an important consideration. As well, one of the reasons for the use of a very limited number of substrates carrying or embodying scenes from the novel was technological: the manufacturers of *Pamela*-related material culture could not as yet utilize reproductive processes to copy existing illustrations onto other materials such as textiles and ceramics. These technologies became available only two decades after the publication of the novel. In this respect, the transmedial use of the same text-evocative images on different media was mainly limited to the faithful reproduction of paintings as engravings: the canvases of Francis Hayman and Joseph Highmore, for example, were respectively reproduced as book illustrations and furniture prints (Keymer and Sabor, 2005, pp. 159–61, pp. 163–5). As Aaron Gabriel Montalvo notes, these 'transform[ed] the interiority of the novel into external appearances' (Montalvo, 2022, p. 28). In these instances of transmediation, artists did not alter the original design in such a way as to affect how a painterly image of the work could be read. The original was translated from a painted, polychrome work on canvas into a reproducible and monochrome, paper-based medium. This reproduction allowed broader familiarity with the designs through the multiplication of copies; at the same time, it functioned within the paratextually defined framework of the illustrated codex, or the print could feature a panel at the bottom providing explanatory text.

This section will examine two instances of the adaptive transmediation of *Pamela* illustrations, the first involving an enamel artisan's altering and transferring of a design onto a substrate – copper – that could not as yet be printed on mechanically. The second instance of transmediation involved the use of an illustration that has not hitherto been discussed by Richardson scholars, an adaptation from its British original to feature in an American edition of *Pamela*. This adaptation entailed a process of visual repurposing and alteration that reflected the publisher's 'desire' for 'the repetition [of the image] as much as the change' (Hutcheon, 2012, p. 9). Importantly, we see the original design moving from one kind of book (a full-text edition) to another (a chapbook) and in the process being shaped by these book formats' cultural status. I argue that the technological limitations to reproduce existing illustrations of Richardson's work mechanically on only a small number of substrates in the mid-eighteenth century reduced the range of objects that could be endowed with transmediated illustrative meaning, unless illustrations were applied by hand. Naturally, objects not embellished with visualizations of *Pamela* through engraving technologies gained value as unique, collectible items. In promoting literary-material meaning and adapted to the use of the new medium on which they featured, their illustrations invoked a fashionable culture of dress and genre scenes that could signify more widely than solely in relation to *Pamela*: the work had to be inferred by those recognizing the illustration. In contrast to the use of a transmediated illustration on an exclusive medium, the adaptation of an English illustration by a late eighteenth-century American publisher using a text technology that differed from the one originally deployed facilitated the production of a widely available (albeit significantly changed) book illustration. I shall demonstrate that the opportunistic, cost-effective recycling of the illustration for both an edition of *Pamela* and another title issued by the same publisher reveals not only the malleability but also the complete non-fixity of representational–illustrative meaning when conditioned by new contexts.

There are only two examples where images by the French artist Hubert-François Gravelot, devised for the upmarket 1742 illustrated edition of *Pamela*, were transmediated onto non–paper-based objects. These examples, not previously studied by Richardson scholars, comprise hand-painted enamelled snuff boxes, 'novelty' objects and some of 'the most appealing of all the delicate products of Georgian craftsmanship' that, from the late 1740s, frequently reproduced embellishments based on French designs (Benjamin, 1999, p. 9). The first image featured Gravelot's rendering of Pamela kneeling at her husband's feet, while the latter shows him remonstrating with his incensed sister, Lady Davers (Watney, 1972, p. 825). A luxury object, this snuff box introduced viewers to a scene in which Pamela, now Mrs B, meets her sister-in-law, who does not credit her brother's statement that he has married their late mother's maid. It is a scene in which we not only see the prejudices of the upper classes projected onto Pamela but also where Pamela's goodness of heart and her desire to avoid a breach between brother and sister are highlighted. Another Gravelot design, Pamela accompanied by Mr B and meeting Miss Godwin, Mr B's illegitimate daughter, appears on the base of an enamelled snuff box, the transmedial meaning of the whole object complicated by the additional ornamentation of two painted designs relating to pastoral amusement.[3]

The transmedial use of the second illustration involves a process of adaptation by which Gravelot's changed design enters into a new medial relationship with the other images on the snuff box (Figures 5 and 6). This new context of intramedial relations results in a rewriting of the literary illustration's meaning because this visualization no longer functions exclusively or even predominantly as an epitext of *Pamela* – unless recognized as such by the beholder of the design. As part of the transmediation of Gravelot's illustration, the artisan realizing the design in enamel has removed the scene from the interior of a gentrified dairy, where the meeting takes place, to a vaguely pastoral setting

---

[3] The snuff box (plate 179d) is reproduced in Watney (1975), p. 275.

Figure 5 Copper-engraved book illustration of '[Pamela meeting Miss Godwin, Mr B. looking on]' (12.7 × 7.5 cm), designed and engraved by H.-F. Gravelot, *Pamela: or Virtue Rewarded* (London: S. Richardson, 1742). Collection Sandro Jung.

Figure 6 Redacted version of H.-F. Gravelot's '[Pamela meeting Miss Godwin, Mr B. looking on]' painted onto an enamel snuff box. Courtesy of the English Ceramic Circle.

framed by a tree on the right. Applied to the inside base of the snuff box, Gravelot's illustration was meant for private viewing, allowing the beholder access to a staged scene that no longer forms part of the sequence of plates that

Hayman and Gravelot had prepared for Richardson's edition. The snuffbox had to be open to reveal the original scene that highlighted Pamela allowing Miss Godwin to become part of her family, an intimate moment that now, in the process of transmediation, translates into a romantic encounter between two lovers. Read as part of a cumulative decorative-illustrative programme embellishing the snuff box, the altered Gravelot image in its new medial setting evokes a new storyworld that could still loosely connect with that of *Pamela*, especially since such an elite object would have involved its own story of production and marketing.

Without appropriate knowledge to identify the design as an epitext of *Pamela*, however, the scene would have represented a depiction of a family in a vaguely pastoral setting. The illustration strips any cues to direct a reading in relation to Richardson's novel. It no longer evokes the narrative of Miss Godwin's origin and related questions of morality; clearly, viewers of the original illustration would only be aware of this element of the story if they had read the text that the plate visualized. Even so, the adaptation of the illustration and its deracination from its textual origin does not mean that viewers would not have recognized that Gravelot had reversed a traditional, pyramidically constructed genre scene constellation by placing Pamela at the centre of the group. By doing so, he positioned her as the person with the ability to bring about the family union between father and illegitimate daughter that Mr B had not done (Shepherd, 2010, p. 90). In doing so, the artist empowered Pamela in a way that would have been recognized by female purchasers of the snuff box especially.

The reach of the transmediated Gravelot image would have been limited, of course, because the expensive object onto which it had been painted would not have circulated widely. The identification of the scene featuring Pamela, Mr B and Miss Godwin depended on an inter-iconic connection to be made with one illustration issued in Richardson's sixth edition, and this edition – priced at £1 4s – was out of the reach of most people. By the late eighteenth century, however, a 'truly elegant and original'[4] illustration of *Pamela* had appeared in a widely available London edition, issued in weekly six-penny numbers. This illustration was subsequently altered, executed as a woodcut and transmediated in American abridgments of the work. The adaptation of the original design made possible new readings of the female character depicted, which in turn shaped readers' understanding of not only Richardson's work but also another one.

Unlike English publishers, in order to supply books that a broad customer base could afford, American publishers at the end of the eighteenth century

---

[4] *Morning Chronicle*, 10 December 1781.

issued abridged versions of *Pamela*, reprinting Francis Newbery's 1769 bowd-
lerized adaptation of Richardson's work. This version of *Pamela* substantively
rewrote Richardson's original by 'turn[ing] ... the first part of the novel into
a condemnatory study of sexual harassment, domestic violence and rape'
(Bannet, 2011, p. 133) and by elucidating Goodman Andrews's once 'easy
circumstances' (Richardson, 1796, p. 5) and his subsequent change of fortune.
As a result of her father's prior social status, as Eve Tavor Bannet has noted,
'Pamela could credibly be virtuous in the manner of girls in the propertied
classes because she was both born and educated into them' (Bannet, 2011,
p. 133). In contrast to Richardson, Newbery 'insisted that the virtuous thing for
a maidservant [molested by her employer] to do was to save herself by running
away' (Bannet, 2011, p. 135). Yet John Lodge, the illustrator employed for
Newbery's edition, did not depart from modes of presenting Pamela sanctioned
by Richardson. His illustrations for Newbery's abridgement, with the exception
of the frontispiece, visualized scenes that had been illustrated in the 1740s,
including Pamela at the pond and her overturning the table on recognizing her
father. His 'Pamela is not a Rococo, stylized female deriving from a canvas:
there is "an earthy quality to his Pamela" that makes her similar to the numerous
simple, at times naively depicted females that populate the title pages of
traditional chapbooks' (Jung, 2016a, p. 523).

   Significantly, Lodge's illustrations were reprinted in chapbooks, at times as
copperplates and at other times as woodcuts by Isaiah Thomas and Samuel Hall
in 1794 and 1797 respectively. The composition of these illustrations did not
alter, however, even though the use of the text technology of the woodcut related
the images to a tradition of cheap print. Publishers' use of format and text
technologies catered to particular book-related literacy, and the materiality of
the chapbook 'anticipat[ed] ... the conditions of its reception', for a book's
material make-up and 'formats index a hoped-for audience' (McGill, 2018,
p. 672, p. 677). Aiming for consistent standards of material realization as well as
the alignment of individual parts of the codex, both typographical and engraved,
ensured that a print form such as a chapbook was easily recognized. For this
reason, rather than reprinting (as opposed to adapting) an existing visualization
of Pamela, New York printer and publisher John Tiebout had an English
illustration adapted, and he would use this reworked image as the frontispiece
for editions of two works that he issued as part of his series of 'Neat Editions
of ... Chapman's Books' in 1796.[5] He reissued the *Pamela* abridgement,
accompanied by the frontispiece, in 1798. In that year the frontispiece image

---

[5] A listing of the titles of his chapbooks occurs as an advertisement sheet inserted in the American
Antiquarian Society copy of Alexander Pope's *An Essay on Man* (New York: printed by John
Tiebout, for E. Duyckinck & Co., 1796).

was also reused in a New York edition printed for Cornelius Davis by T. Kirk, the printer who had also executed Tiebout's edition.

This section will consider the transmedial transformation for use on a distinct cheap print book form of Edward Burney's illustration of Pamela showing her new country dress and straw hat to Mrs Jervis. It was the third plate in a series of sixteen that the artist furnished for the twentieth volume of James Harrison's *Novelist's Magazine* in 1785. This series of engravings had introduced six scenes, including the one to be discussed, that had not previously been selected for visualization. I shall examine how Burney's design was altered by replacing the original domestic context of the illustration for use in Tiebout's New York editions of *The History of Pamela; or, Virtue Rewarded* (co-published with Edward O'Brien) and *The History of Fair Rosamond, Mistress of Henry II, and Jane Shore, Concubine to Edward IV. Kings of England* (Figures 7 and 8). The American engraver embedded

Figure 7 Copper-engraved book illustration of E. Burney's '[Pamela in her Country Dress presenting herself to Mrs Jervis]' (17.6 × 11.2 cm), *Pamela: or, Virtue Rewarded* (London: Harrison and Co., 1785). Collection Sandro Jung.

Figure 8 Wood-engraving of redacted design of Burney's '[Pamela in her
Country Dress presenting herself to Mrs Jervis]', *The History of Pamela; or,
Virtue Rewarded* (New York: Tiebout and O'Brien, 1796). Reproduced courtesy
of the American Antiquarian Society.

Burney's Pamela in a new setting to serve as a meaningful frontispiece for
either of Tiebout's titles.

In copying Burney's figure, the American engraver reverses the design,
the most direct mode of reproducing the image onto the engraving substrate.
But he retains the details of the English artist's accurate visual translation of
the description of Pamela's 'Country-Habit' that she furnishes for her parents: '[I] put on my round-ear'd ordinary Cap; but with a green Knot . . ., my
home-spun Gown and Petticoat, and plain-leather Shoes . . . and my ordinary
Hose. . . . A plain Muslin Tucker I put on, and my black Silk Necklace . . . and
when I was quite 'quipp'd, I took my Straw Hat in my Hand, with its two blue
Strings' (Richardson, 2011, p. 51). These 'Cloaths', as Pamela intimates to
Mrs Jervis, are 'suitable to my Condition'. In their simplicity, moreover,
they contrast with the expensive silk dresses that her late mistress had given
her. Due to the cheaper text technology of the woodcut employed for
Tiebout's frontispiece, which could not reproduce the fineness of lines and
nuanced tonality of the copper engraving, not all of the details can be as
easily identified as in James Heath's copper engraving of Burney's design.

The plate for Harrison had captured Mrs Jervis's surprise at seeing Pamela 'thus metamorphos'd', for she initially did not recognize her favourite until the latter identified herself. The moment represented by Burney precedes the identification and follows Richardson's detail that the housekeeper 'pull'd off her spectacles' before inquiring what the unrecognized Pamela might want with her. Burney's illustration anticipates Pamela's return home to re-join her parents in order to avoid Mr B's immodest attentions. It refers to a future life in which the dress Mrs Jervis studies carefully represents a version of Pamela's 'grey Russet', the 'poor honest Dress' that she wore when first arriving in Lady B's household (Richardson 2011, p. 22). The maiden admits to her parents that her new dress 'may look but poor to what I have been us'd to wear of late Days, yet it will serve me, when I am with you, for a good Holiday and Sunday Suit' (Richardson 2011, p. 42). It will thus suit her condition as a virtuous girl from her social class.

In the process of adapting the English plate, the American engraver moves Pamela from her decentred position to the centre. The reworking of the original plate not only involves the removal of Mrs Jervis but also the close, text-interpretive connection that Burney's design made with a specific vignette from the novel. For Tiebout's plate, situating Richardson's heroine in a landscape where she is flanked by a tree and a farm dwelling in the background does not appear to visualize a concrete situation from the narra-tive that forms part of a longer vignette. Rather, it may, as a consequence of Mr B's harassment, constitute an escapist fantasy on the part of Pamela: she imagines her return to a way of life that she left behind when leaving her parents. For reader-viewers of the New York illustration unfamiliar with Burney's design, the storyworld of the scene rendered for the *Novelist's Magazine* will not be inferred. Nor will be Mr B's interactions with Goodman Andrews's daughter, the latter driving Pamela's wish to leave her master's household. Instead, Tiebout's version of the plate may remind reader-viewers of the reprinted frontispiece from Newbery's design. That illustration also depicted Pamela in a similar setting (Figure 9). In contrast to Burney's design, moreover, the set of plates for Newbery's abridgement of *Pamela* of which this frontispiece formed a part was aimed at a different audience: those people with less buying power, including young readers.

And yet given its transmedial dynamics, another reading altogether is pos-sible. In one additional respect, Burney's realization of Pamela differs from the New York frontispiece because in the latter Pamela is no longer smiling. The unhappy facial expression and the setting make possible a reading of the plate that captures a particular moment on her way to her confinement at the Lincolnshire estate: 'at last [Robin, the coach driver,] stopped at a farm

Figure 9 Copper engraving depicting Pamela, *The History of Pamela; or, Virtue Rewarded* (Worcester: Isaiah Thomas, 1794). Reproduced courtesy of the American Antiquarian Society.

house, where she had never been before. Amazed and affrighted, she sought to make the people of the house her friends; but they were Mr B's tenants' (Richardson, 1796, p. 20). If the happy and playful scene of Burney's design has indeed been transformed into a moment of distress – Pamela not being assisted by anyone in her plight – then this remediation of the illustration signifies a complete recasting of the heroine.

While the plate for the *Novelist's Magazine* did not feature a caption that glossed the subject depicted, Tiebout's *Pamela* abridgement furnished the heroine's name in capitals, 'PAMELA', at the bottom of the frontispiece but without any paratextual cues on how to read the character and setting represented. Pamela's name was reproduced by means of set type, which could be printed cost-effectively at the same time as the woodcut, thus allowing Tiebout the reuse of the woodcut for *The History of Fair Rosamond* where only the subject's name, 'FAIR ROSAMOND', as well as the lines of verse underneath,

Figure 10 Wood-engraving of redacted version of frontispiece to *The History of Pamela* (New York, 1796), *The History of Fair Rosamond ... and Jane Shore* (New York: J. Tiebout, 1796). Reproduced courtesy of the American Antiquarian Society.

needed to be set (Figure 10).[6] Reading the addition of Pamela's name to the frontispiece as a confirmation of the character's recognized status as 'a renowned and heroic figure despite the fact that she was entirely fictional' (Walsh, 2017, p. 154), Megan Walsh assigns text-related specificity and particularity to the image, seeing it as one uniquely attuned to and illustrative of Pamela only. Walsh's taking for granted that the image is not derivative and can function only in the specific context of Tiebout's abridgement runs counter to the printer's illustration practice and his transmediating the same illustration for use in his edition of *The History of the Fair Rosamond.*

---

[6] The type was reset for the 1798 printing of the frontispiece to accompany Tiebout's second edition of *The History of Pamela*, and at that point it featured two ornamental devices on each side of Pamela's name that differed from those ones used in 1796.

The opportunistic reuse of the frontispiece to Tiebout's edition of *The History of Pamela* in his edition of *The History of Fair Rosamond* was, of course, cost-saving. He issued the edition once his business partnership ended in May 1796, likely driven by the performance that month, in Philadelphia and elsewhere, of Thomas Hull's 1774 tragedy, *King Henry II, or, the Fall of Fair Rosamond*.[7] In reinscribing an image depicting the moral paragon Pamela with Rosamond's identity, the publisher visually cast two fundamentally different characters in the same way. In serving as a frontispiece to the latter's history, therefore, the illustration no longer represents a chaste young woman but the twelfth-century royal mistress, Rosamond Clifford. In addition to the name of Henry II's mistress – and to aid comprehension of the figure as a repentant individual – four lines of verse are given: 'To be the best beloved of a King, / I vainly thought to be so great a Thing, / That I, to gratify his lustful Pleasure, / To his Embraces gave my Virgin Treasure.' These lines draw attention to Rosamond's vanity and ambition as motivation for her to become the King's mistress. At the same time, they give voice to the recognition that her 'Virgin Treasure' was given thoughtlessly and without consideration of the consequences. The Rosamond of the illustration, similar to the Pamela of Tiebout's edition, is characterized by sadness: her lips convey her melancholy and her sense of the gravity of the loss of 'her good name, fame and chastity' (*Fair Rosamond*, 1796, p. 16). This revision of the facial expression that characterized Burney's Pamela when talking to Mrs Jervis thus also captures the mental state of the 'unfortunate Rosamond' (*Fair Rosamond*, 1796, p. 6).

The inter-iconic connection between the frontispieces to Tiebout's editions of *The History of Pamela* and *The History of Fair Rosamond* would be recognized by readers familiar with both volumes. In fact, Tiebout's edition invites a reading of Rosamond that applies the moral standards extolled by Richardson. Even though the frontispiece depicting Henry II's mistress casts her as a deterring example of the kind Pamela resisted when rebuffing Mr B's advances, the editor's preface insists that Rosamond's history should be understood as a didactic work that highlights the danger of temptation. It instructs readers to 'avoid the occasion of sin; for here, they shall see, lust is a pleasure bought with pain, a delight hatch'd with disquiet, a contend [sic] pass'd with fear, and a sin finish'd with sorrow' (*Fair Rosamond*, 1796, p. 9). The preface offers a sympathetic view of Rosamond, and the narrative that follows reveals her as a victim of the King's machinations to possess her. There are repeated

---

[7] The dissolution of the business partnership was announced in *The Diary or London's Register*, 2 January 1797, whereas the performance of Hull's play was advertised in *American Citizen*, 2 May 1796. Nicholas Rowe's *Jane Shore* had been performed from February to April that year, first in Philadelphia and subsequently in New York.

parallels between Pamela and Fair Rosamond, the admonitions offered to the latter by her father closely echoing Goodman Andrews's warnings. Since chastity essentially defines a young woman of 'honour', explanations of the meaning of 'unlawful love' and 'lust' (*Fair Rosamond*, 1796, p. 26) operate to impress upon Rosamond the inestimable value of her 'virtue'. Virtue, of course, must always be on guard. Alethea, 'Rosamond's false governess' (*Fair Rosamond*, 1796, p. 30), conspires against the Clifford family: she abuses the trust Rosamond's father reposes in her when removing his daughter to Cornwall, a place to live in seclusion and unmolested by the King. Alethea, having apprised Henry of Rosamond's whereabouts, frustrates this measure. The governess is handsomely paid by the King for her assistance in corrupting Rosamond, and it is she who, resembling Mrs Jewkes, devises a plan for Henry to rape her charge, Alethea's place in bed with Rosamond being supplied by the King. In marked contrast to Pamela, however, Rosamond does not resist the King's embraces. In spite of portraying Rosamond's vanity and ambition, the narrator at the end of the tale nevertheless regards her as a victim who was 'led astray by the glittering tinsels of royalty' (*Fair Rosamond*, 1796, p. 78) and who paid the price by being poisoned by Queen Eleanor.

Significantly, the frontispiece image features Rosamond humbled, for she has been removed from the royal court. No longer 'dressed . . . with all the gallantry imaginable, according to the mode of that age' (*Fair Rosamond*, 1796, p. 39), but in simple country garb, she appears to have retired, probably to Woodstock, where she would meet her untimely end. The regret voiced in the lines of verse below the image does not reflect the tale that follows because she does not reproach Henry but is beloved by him. Standing as she is in the setting that would have befitted Pamela's originary status, her lament contrasts with the innocence of the idyllic background. The simplicity of dress and of the environment can neither conceal her unhappiness, nor are they causally related to it. Readers recognizing that the illustration used for Pamela was reused to represent Rosamond will imaginatively introduce the character of Richardson's work. The transmedial process of reading Henry II's mistress as a fallen Pamela projects a fate that Pamela would have suffered had she given in to Mr B's advances. This inter-iconic connection between Tiebout's editions of *The History of Pamela* and *The History of Fair Rosamond* allows a reading that inflects the meaning-making of the frontispiece to the latter title with knowledge of the moral issues at stake in the former. The manner in which the visualized Rosamond is glossed by the lines underneath the image represents an instance of transmedia storytelling in which the reader opening the volume meets with a characterization of the young woman that the text that follows does not support. It thus represents an extra-textual device of meaning-making that supports the editor's prefatory moralizing agenda.

The transmedial transformation of Burney's design by Tiebout involved a new context in which the image of Pamela was made to signify in fundamentally different ways from the English artist's original intention to capture a specific vignette from Richardson's work. Critically, its visual revision and realization as a woodcut for a materially different medium made it affordable to a broader audience than would have been able to purchase Harrison's *Novelist's Magazine* edition. The chapbook format in which Tiebout issued *The History of Pamela* and *The History of Fair Rosamond*, furthermore, underpinned the titles' didactic-moralizing intent. By contrast, Harrison's plates had offered a more wide-ranging visual interpretation focused on vignettes that were not explicitly moralizing and did not require reader-viewers to reflect on the reasons for Pamela's sadness highlighted in Tiebout's frontispiece.

The visual revision of Burney's illustration entailed a change in representational modality, transforming the central character from a happy maiden delighted at surprising Mrs Jervis with her new 'Country-Habit' into a dejected individual no longer part of the interior social spaces of affluence that had previously characterized her existence. Arguably, though, levels of interpretive response would not be static. While many reader-viewers in America would have been able to apprehend the iconically rendered sadness of Pamela and Rosamond, only a small, select group of elite individuals would have been able to resituate in a prior reading of Richardson's work the pastoral scene on the snuff box into which Gravelot's engraved genre painting had been transformed. This casting of the French artist's scene in idyllic terms, portraying a supposedly prelapsarian notion of innocence, relies, of course, on an illusion because Miss Godwin was conceived out of wedlock and thus tainted with sin. It is Pamela's ability to forgive Mr B and her willingness to adopt his daughter as her own that will ensure a happy life as a family for them. But, removed from the moral framework of the codex as part of which Gravelot's illustration functioned, the reductive rendering on the snuff box allows a reading that centralizes Pamela and does not foreground Mr B's transgressions.

As we can now appreciate, the transmediation of existing illustrations involves processes of reproduction, by hand or mechanically, facilitated by different text technologies and on different substrates. As well, it recreates meaning through visual revision and remediation, a process that appropriates the visual image to new contexts, ideologies and audiences, as well as materials. The adaptation of Burney's illustration for Tiebout's edition of *Pamela* highlighted a melancholy that is frequently expressed in the young woman's letters but not illustrated in any other edition. Rendering Pamela as sad bestows individuality on her, since it invokes experience that will have led to the feeling conveyed by her facial expression. The transmediated image does not fundamentally change the way in which Richardson's novel can be understood, but it creates a new emphasis, a public image of the effects of suffering experienced in private that, until the appearance of Tiebout's edition, had not been introduced iconically to reader-viewers.

3 Damon, Musidora and the Containment of Desire: From Vase to Miniature

In the transmedial adaptation of illustrations, the changing of scale and focus alters the readability and meaning of an image. Necessarily, artisans undertake omissions of human figures, as well as the visual recasting of these individuals, for specific reasons. They represent strategies to appropriate existing visual illustrations of literary characters and scenes to contexts that cater to particular occasions; issues of propriety and morality must be taken into account in order to avoid or prevent any offence and, at the same time, to maximize the enhanced hybrid meaning of the object featuring an illustration. The following case study of illustrations of the Damon and Musidora tale from Thomson's 'Summer' illuminates how changes made to illustrations as part of transmediation involve both scale and focus. We see not only the omission of a human being from the composition but also significant visual rewriting. The tale introduces a scene in which a young maiden, Musidora, is readying herself for a bath in a concealed woodland setting; as she undresses, her lover, Damon, accidentally finds himself near her and watches her disrobing. His delicacy compels him to flee the scene but not before he has left a note to reveal to his beloved that he has witnessed her denuding. In the eighteenth and nineteenth centuries, Thomson's tale was ambivalently understood in terms of the eroticism of Damon's voyeurism and the poet's insistence on Musidora's innocence, an ambivalence Ralph Cohen has identified in castings of Musidora alternately as 'nude' and as 'prude' (Cohen, 1964, p. 294). This examination of the transmediation of iconic 'refractions' (Colombo, 2014, p. 402) of the story will explore the erotic aesthetics of visualizations and the ways in which their adaptation on other media manipulated the meanings of the original printed designs of these iconizations.

My discussion will focus on two engravings of the lovers by, respectively, the Swiss-born Angelica Kauffman and by William Hamilton and examine how these visualizations were adapted for use on two upmarket media: a Duesbury porcelain vase and an enamel miniature. Kauffman's design introduced the lovers to late eighteenth-century collectors of prints; however, the artisan appropriating Kauffman's image did not merely copy this print but also altered it for application on the vase. I shall examine why the artisan responsible for transferring Kauffman's design opted to alter central elements of this erotically charged scene of voyeurism, arguing that in a public, representational object such as the vase, the Thomsonian eroticism required muting through re-inscription. By contrast, I shall argue that in the transmedial use of Hamilton's book illustration on an enamel miniature, a new focus created for the image necessitates, because of the space constraints of the medial carrier and consequent rescaling, the elimination of background detail and intra-iconic interpersonal connections. The deracination of the image from the context of the printed edition for use on an object as private as an erotic miniature also replaces the intermedial dynamic of looking and reading by which the illustration was defined as part of the codex. It requires a new, relational mode of apprehension that centres on the erotic body and on the associations that the name of Musidora evoked in the viewer's mind. Rather than focus exclusively on the bi-medial text–image relationship according to which the printed image serves as an embodied version of Thomson's poetic narrative, my discussion of the use of these images on other media assigns the medium 'inherent' and 'attached' value (Prown, 1982, p. 3). As such, it becomes an object of cultural meaningfulness because it shapes iconic meaning and serves through its materiality as a connection to the object culture of conspicuous consumption. As I will demonstrate, this varied material culture requires practices of meaning-making that facilitate an understanding of the subjects depicted visually on their own terms but also in conjunction with the associated function of the object that they embellish. The whole functions as medium of textual recall that encourages the reimagination of Thomson's Damon and Musidora.

Among individually issued prints of the Damon and Musidora tale, the one that James Birchall published in 1782 as part of a pair, the second print depicting Thomson's 'Celadon and Amelia', proved particularly popular.[8] Angelica Kauffman had produced a small-scale painting, a cabinet picture 'in the possession of Mr. Snelling', on which the oval print (measuring 24.1 × 18.5 cm and available in versions printed in black and brown) was based. The design found application on other media, too, including as coloured oval panels on furniture, such as on a table undertaken by the Braunschweig firm of Stobwasser in c. 1790.[9] It was furthermore used on a secretaire commode manufactured by George Brookshaw, a furniture painter and japanner, in c. 1785–90.[10] The panels would have provided additional attractions to visitors viewing these customized pieces of furniture. In 1783–4, the Derby firm of William Duesbury also utilized Kauffman's Damon and Musidora design on a large and spectacular soft-paste porcelain vase that had the design

---

[8] *Caledonian Mercury*, 25 March 1782. The set of prints retailed at 12s.

[9] Braunschweiger Lackkunst (werkverzeichnis-stobwasser.de).

[10] The Lady Lever Art Gallery, Liverpool.

realized in painted enamel and gilt.[11] Each material medium-illustration entity possessed 'inherent factors' that, according to Lars Elleström, shape an object's semiotic modality, especially in terms of its iconicity and symbolicity (Elleström, 2019, p. 46, p. 48). These objects, even though they featured similar versions of Kauffman's design, functioned differently from one another, the 'desire-induced symbols' (Scarpaci, 2016, p. 8) of the medial hybrid invoking practices and processes of meaning-making that depended on the unique specificity of the process of mediation between material artefact and its visual inscription.

Kauffman's design embellishes the central vase of a three-piece Derby garniture, the other pieces being ewers decorated with Shakespearean scenes (Figures 11 and 12).[12] Featuring on the 'therm vase', 'a hybrid Antique

Figure 11 Sepia print of 'Damon and Musidora' (24.1 × 18.5 cm), designed by Angelica Kauffman, engraved by Francesco Bartolozzi (London: James Birchall, 1782). Collection Sandro Jung.

---

[11] Victoria and Albert Museum Victoria (museum number: C.263–1935) and Victoria and Albert Museum (museum number: 825:1, 2–1882).
[12] British Museum (museum number: 1923,1218.13.CR).

Figure 12 Enamel painting of an adapted design of Kauffman's design of 'Damon and Musidora', Derby Porcelain Vase (height: 40.64 cm). British Museum number: 1923,1218.13CR. Courtesy of the Trustees of the British Museum.

form, with handles of winged harpies' (Ferguson, 2018, p. 26), Kauffman's scene conveys its story through a neoclassical medium to illustrate a classic modern subject. The three components of the garniture entailed the framing of the large vase by the ewers and in the process relate Thomson's work to Shakespeare's canonical productions. In this respect, the garniture promoted the monumentalization of Thomson through an elite ceramic medium, his poem – represented through Kauffman's rendering of the Musidora story – being physically flanked by visualizations of Shakespeare's works. This multi-piece garniture not only entailed a particular spatial arrangement of the individual porcelain objects to create a pyramidic scene but also, by means of the caryatid handles of the central vase – through the association of caryatids (or korai [maidens]) with the maidens who carried sacred goods used at feasts of the gods – imbued it with a proto-sacral function. The symbolism of the caryatid handles shapes the material meaning of the object as a vessel – akin to a Greek illustrated vase – to tell a mythological or sacred story. The three strands of pearls underneath each of the handles furthermore support the symbolism of purity, innocence and virginity that the image and text infer separately but also interconnectedly. At the same time, the set of vase and ewers were display objects that functioned simultaneously as status symbols that spoke to the currency of the owner's cultural taste and discrimination.

The large painted oval panel containing Kauffman's design introduced a clothed (but undressing) Musidora, in the process of dipping her left foot into the water. The artist captured a moment that precedes the one usually adopted in visual representations of the tale: Musidora nude. In contrast to all earlier renderings of Musidora, Kauffman's version is not a statuesque, disrobed and standing, Venus-like figure, a model introduced by Thomson when he likened Musidora to 'the statue that enchants the world' (1342).[13] Rather, she is seated while disrobing, oblivious to anyone's invasion of her privacy. With downcast eyes, she is smilingly removing a cestus-like garment, which functions as both the love-inspiring cestus of Venus (Thomson's 'virgin zone' [1305]) and a device to secure her 'loose[ly] array[ed]' (1286) robe. The loosened dress already reveals her right breast but still covers most of her legs. The colours chosen for Musidora's clothing – purple, pink and cream, as well as their symbolic meanings – underscore her nobility and sophistication but also her sensuousness. In this image, she functions as an erotic icon capable of firing the imagination, yet she is also chaste and innocent, unaware of Damon's voyeurism.

I argue that Thomson created an analogy between Musidora and chaste goddesses such as Venus (Aphrodite Urania) and (by invoking the judgement of Paris on Mount Ida) Hera and Athena to characterize her as an ideal beauty. However, the adaptor of Kauffman's image could not rely on the mnemonic presence of these intertextual meanings. For that reason, he devised visual strategies to reduce associations of immodesty, highlighting instead Damon's 'delicate refinement' (1291) and 'love's respectful modesty' (1320) in his viewing his lover. In the process, the remediation of Birchall's intaglio printed design on the vase entailed a visual rewriting of the relationship between the two lovers. The principal but highly significant difference between the 1782 print and the adaptation of the design for the vase occurs because the distance between the two lovers has been increased in the revision of the image for the porcelain object. The print had represented Musidora and Damon positioned so closely that Damon's leg almost touches the rock on which his lover is seated. Damon's sightline directly leads to Musidora's breast, although her position, facing away from him, makes it impossible that he could possibly see the breast. Even so, his eyes

---

[13] All references to Thomson's 'Summer' will be by parenthetical line number and based on James Sambrook's 1981 edition of *The Seasons*.

direct the individual contemplating Musidora's uncovered bosom and invite the viewing that Damon cannot perform.

Musidora and Damon clearly were designed as part of one group, even though the viewer of the print needed to suspend disbelief and take for granted that the former was not aware of the latter's presence. By contrast, on the vase Damon appears much further away from Musidora, which is indicated by not only the physical distance between the two figures but also the size of his figure. Arguably, the image on the vase introduces a decorous scene in which Damon appears more respectful than in the print. In fact, the revision of Kauffman's design resulted in the compositional creation of two distinct figures who were no longer part of the central group devised by the artist. Appearing forward and confident in the print, Damon appears decidedly more boy-like in the way that he is realized on the vase, thereby reducing the erotic frisson of the composition of the print. The boy-Damon of the vase is not characterized by the 'ebon tresses' of Thomson's swimming youth, introduced right before the Damon and Musidora tale commences (which Birchall's print had featured); instead, he boasts a short haircut that is not expressive of the virility associated with long male hair. One striking difference between the print and the design on the vase is the introduction of a willow behind Damon: at the start of Thomson's tale, Damon is described as 'pierc'd with love's delightful pangs' 'Among the bending willows' (1271, 1274). Kauffman had omitted the willow tree. The willow serves to define Damon less erotically than in the print; moreover, the artisan responsible for the design on the vase positioned the tree closely to Damon because the symbolism of the willow implied chastity and purity, qualities that contribute to muting the boy-Damon's erotic sensations when chancing upon Musidora.

In contrast to the visual strategies adopted for the remediated Kauffman design on the vase, a text-defined strategy helped to direct meaning-making in relation to the scene of Birchall's print. While on the level of representation the print introduced a scene of voyeurism and male curiosity, the accompanying caption did not reference Damon, except through the possessive pronoun 'his':

> For, lo conducted by the laughing Loves,
> This cool retreat his Musidora sought:
> Warm in her cheek the sultry season glow'd,
> And rob'd in loose Array, she came to bathe
> Her fervent limbs in the refreshing stream.
>
> ('Summer', 1287–91)

The caption text thus obscured Damon's presence, as well as his writing the letter. At the same time, only those observers with textual knowledge of the tale will have been able to understand Damon's invasive presence. The actual representation of the two characters on the vase effectively brings together two distinct moments in the design that, in Thomson's story, remained temporally distinct: Musidora's undressing and Damon's writing a letter to his beloved. Thus, the viewer of the two versions of Kauffman's design, both in the print and repurposed on the vase, is not granted a look at the fully nude Musidora, the invasion of whose privacy induces Damon to leave the scene. Because Damon records his having observed Musidora in his letter, the look is anticipated only and not yet accomplished, thus raising questions related to meanings (concerning Damon's holding a pen, for instance) that anyone without knowledge of Thomson's tale would need to contemplate.

The Duesbury artisan's decision to adapt Kauffman's design in such a way that it reimagined the relationship between the two figures depicted reflected the firm's marketing the garniture as an object of display that likely featured as part of a table setting. Its public viewing contrasted with the more private format of Birchall's print, the oval print being understood as a cabinet picture of much smaller scale than a large-scale furniture print. Whereas Birchall had sought to frame meaning paratextually through the lines of poetry that minimized Damon's presence at the scene, it was the Duesbury artisan's recasting of Damon as a boy rather than as a lover fired by sexual arousal that emphasized the innocence of the scene and, in particular, Musidora's chastity. By contrast, another version published as a print by W. Dickinson in 1787 presents a Musidora who has now bared both her breasts and a Damon attentively observing her undressing rather than writing his letter to her. The latter print no longer reproduces lines of poetry: it therefore does not direct meaning or furnish a textual guide to how Musidora's undressing should be understood in the context of Damon's voyeurism. Dickinson's print elaborated the eroticism of Kauffman's design, whereas the material framing of her illustration by the artisan responsible for the modelling of the Duesbury vase reduced its eroticism. Even though Kauffman's design visualizes a modern subject, he puts this image into dialogue with the classical tradition through the caryatid handles and through their symbolic inscription. The realization of the design of the vase is framed by flowers that invoke the pastoralism of innocence that the new design of the Damon figure implies. The flowers do not therefore function as pure ornament but contribute modally to the definition of the central oval's meaning.

While Kauffman produced a number of designs for oval prints of scenes from *The Seasons*, William Hamilton (like Kauffman, a Fellow of the Royal Academy) illustrated four editions of *The Seasons* from 1778 to 1815. In so doing, he produced a large repertoire of iconic interpretations. Hamilton's design of the Damon and Musidora tale for Francis Isaac Du Roveray's 1802 subscription edition – which in contrast to Kauffman's design captured a fully nude Musidora – was subsequently remediated: first, by means of a revised version of the illustration for use on the title page of an early nineteenth-century American edition of Thomson's poem; second, on an enamel miniature. The Damon and Musidora tale (which Hamilton had already visualized for editions published in 1778 and 1798) provided one of three subjects that the artist painted for Du Roveray's large octavo edition.

Hamilton's painting had been exhibited at the Royal Academy in 1801. He glossed it as a visualization of a specific passage from Thomson: the ten lines of poetry accompanying the exhibition catalogue description of the painting focus on Damon's 'headlong', hurried departure from the scene and Musidora's subsequent astonishment – 'as if to marble struck' – once she becomes aware of his having observed her disrobing (*1801 Catalogue*, p. 18).[14] The dynamic of Damon's precipitate departure and Musidora's stasis captures the Thomsonian text accurately, but the remediations of Hamilton's design that appeared in America alter the meaning in unintended ways. The significance of this alteration becomes clear when we explore how the removal of Damon's intrusive presence in the transmedial adaptations of Hamilton's design reshaped Musidora's meaning within the landscape but also within the context of the relational medium in which she is viewed.

The appropriation of Hamilton's design for a small book illustration within a more conservative moral American environment, where the nude would not have been understood as part of an artistic convention that linked it to classical statuary, can be shown to have reinforced its potentially questionable moral value. I will argue that, despite strategies involving the removal of Damon and background detail, these repurposed versions of Hamilton's design strengthened their associations with the erotic. At the same time, these adaptations embedded them – through the miniature edition and the enamel miniature – within private consumption practices where even the edition of *The Seasons* may have been easily concealed in a pocket because of its titillating frontispiece.

John Heath's engraved plate of Hamilton's design for Du Roveray is characterized by a density of cross-hatching and roulette work that darkens considerably the area surrounding the figure of Musidora, a contrast that highlights Musidora's centrality at the same time as it functions symbolically to underscore the nude's purity. The design encourages the reader to imagine the eroticism of the Damon and Musidora tale: here, the bare-breasted Musidora in the foreground, one foot in the water already in anticipation of her bath, contrasts with earlier illustrations of

---

[14] The ten-line passage (consisting of lines 1336–9, followed by lines 1343–8) alters Thomson's original by omitting the five lines that record Damon's written message to Musidora.

Drawn by Wm Hamilton R.A.   *Engraved by J. Heath. A.*

Figure 13 Copper-engraved book illustration depicting Damon and Musidora
(22.9 × 15 cm), designed by William Hamilton and engraved by John Heath,
The Seasons (London: F. I. Du Roveray, 1802). Collection Sandro Jung.

the standing nude Musidora where the bather appears shy and apprehensive of
being observed.[15] Hamilton's Musidora faces the viewer unabashedly, her eyes
clearly directed at the person beholding the illustration. But her position is such
that her left leg, slightly raised, obscures a view of her genital area (Figure 13). In
the process of disrobing, she stretches her upper body in such a way that her
breasts project and become the visual focus of her body, resulting in one of the

---

[15] Hamilton's first visualization of the tale for John Murray's 1778 edition rendered her as a nude
who avoids eye contact with the reader-viewer and seeks to present herself as modest by
directing her gaze to the right, covering her breasts and genital area with her hands. David
Pyet's illustration for the 1789 edition for Peter Hill also shows Musidora in profile, not facing
the reader. Johann Sebastian Bach's 1788 print of a design by Johann Friedrich Bause allowed
the viewer a frontal image of Musidora, as did Thomas Stothard for John Stockdale's 1794
edition of *The Seasons*, but both artists emphasize her modesty through gestures meant to cover
her breasts and genital area.

most risqué renderings of the figure produced.[16] In the left-hand background, her lover Damon, who is represented at a third of Musidora's size, is in the process of leaving the scene. His longing glance back at the young woman enhances the eroticism. Musidora's pose, however, obstructs his view of her body through the garment that she is lifting. This titillating scene points to the attractive force of Musidora's erotic body, a full view of which is at once withheld from Damon but granted to the reader-viewer (who does not form part of the intra-iconic realm of the illustration, even though he or she is a participant in the spectacle of Musidora's denuding by being an onlooker).

That this visual version of the tale of Damon and Musidora was potentially offensive to viewers is confirmed by the editor of the 1777 'school' edition of *The Seasons* published in London by J. French: George Wright opined that the tale and specifically 'the too particular description of Musidora undressing herself' were 'extremely disgustful to the modest reader' (Thomson, 1777, p. 206). His view also likely underpinned the adaptation of Hamilton's design for use on the title page of the American 1814 miniature edition issued by Georgetown booksellers Richards and Mallory and their Philadelphia partner, P. H. Nicklin (Figure 14). Wright's objection to Thomson's description of Musidora's undressing was grounded in its visual function, the image fixing a moment in an unfolding story that spectacularizes nudity. Compared to Hamilton's visualization, the plate impression of the design (much reduced in size and measuring 5.4 × 5.8 cm) presents a less erotically charged scene of the 'cool retreat' (1288): now the figure of the voyeur-lover, Damon, has been removed, and on closer inspection it also reveals that the physical plate, which will have been used for an unidentified earlier printing of the illustration, was altered, the figure being manually erased through cross-hatching covering the area previously occupied by Damon (Jung, 2016b, p. 227). So, rather than considering the overt display of Musidora's body offensive and lacking propriety, the individual responsible for the alteration of the copper plate clearly objected to Damon's presence, especially since the artisan responsible for the design of the figure of Damon in the American illustration had not copied Hamilton's fleeing figure. Instead, he had repositioned the (now obscured) lover as a static individual directly facing Musidora, which interprets him as not following the dictates of propriety by removing himself from the scene. The forceful erasure of Damon from the copperplate thus represented the removal of a morally ambiguous element from the composition, forcing the readers' focus on Musidora on her own and as virtuous.

---

[16] Only one other illustration, Conrad Martin Metz's illustration of the scene for Murray's 1792 edition, presented her facing the viewer, her breasts a focal point since she stretches out her arms and her genital area only slightly covered by a garment that she is about to remove.

Figure 14 Adapted copper-engraved book illustration depicting Damon and
Musidora (5.4 × 5.8 cm), designed by William Hamilton and engraved by
G. Fairman (Georgetown: Richards and Mallory, 1814). Collection Sandro Jung.

Richards and Mallory were not the only American bookselling firm to reuse
a British book illustration from which they had the figure of Damon removed. Ten
years before they issued their miniature edition, the Philadelphia publisher
Thomas Dobson had produced his own edition, which reprinted, in reverse,
three other plates that Hamilton had contributed to Du Roveray's edition.
Hamilton's Musidora design was not used by Dobson, however, probably because
of the display of nudity. It was replaced by a design that Thomas Kirk had devised
for an edition published in 1802 by a conger of nineteen London bookselling firms.
The design was strongly reminiscent of Kauffman's visualization, especially since
it introduced a seated Musidora who, though largely clothed, exhibits her upper

body where one breast is already visible. A large tree trunk functions as a wide physical barrier between Musidora in the foreground and Damon in the right-hand background, the latter's sight focused on his lover's half-bare torso. Despite the tree trunk, however, Damon's physical proximity to Musidora is very close. For Dobson's edition, Alexander Lawson's re-engraving of Kirk's design omitted Damon. The added caption, 'Warm in her cheek the sultry season glow'd / And rob'd in loose array, she came to bathe', reinforced the sense of her solitary bathing, no mention being made of Damon.

Even more so than Lawson's, the visual rewriting of Hamilton's design in the frontispiece to Richards and Mallory's edition transformed the scene into one of a decontextualized nude about to bathe. The rounded shape of this title-page vignette incorporates vegetation – trees (including a willow difficult to make out on the left of the vignette) and bushes – in order to create a protective, arbour-like structure that secures Musidora from prying eyes such as Damon's. But even this limited portrayal of a nude was contentious in early nineteenth-century America. As E. McSherry Fowble notes, 'a classical view of the nude in art as a symbol of truth and beauty' (McSherry Fowble, 1974, p. 105) was only beginning to be established at the time. Indeed, Americans still 'viewed the nude as a statement of questionable morality' (McSherry Fowble, 1974, p. 113), and it was as late as 1813 that, on the occasion of the third annual exhibition of the Philadelphia Academy, Charles Leslie's copy of Benjamin West's 'Musidora Bathing' was introduced to an American audience. The move, however, did not on its own establish 'the social propriety of the nude', especially if displayed at a public exhibition (McSherry Fowble, 1974, p. 120).

The reshaping of the background in the frontispiece to the Georgetown edition centralized Musidora in a way that the Philadelphia-based, British-born miniature painter William Russell Birch would utilize for his own recontextualization of Hamilton's design for an enamel miniature on copper.[17] This miniature – which was painted c. 1810 and measures 4.7 × 4.0 cm – proved a popular commodity, and he produced a number of copies as a result (Figure 15).[18] Birch's enamel painting

---

[17] One copy of the miniature, entitled 'Venus' and mounted in a rectangular frame, is held by the Pennsylvania Academy of the Fine Arts (accession number: 1869.4).

[18] See Birch's 'Book of Profitts' (P.2016.50.64) in the Library Company of Philadelphia. In Birch's book of accounts, he lists a number of enamels featuring Venus and 'Musadora', which may depict the same subject. In cost, the cheapest ('a small Venus'), which he sold to a Captain Clark in April 1815 for $10, corresponded to the price he charged respectively for a 'small head' and 'likeness of a Dead Brother'. The price of a miniature, however, depended on whether the miniature was executed on metal or ivory, as well as on whether or not Birch used enamel or water colour. In February 1823 Birch sold another 'Venus' to a Mr Catlin for $30, while, in addition to one disposed of in 1824, two 'Musadoras' sold in October and December 1823, retailing at $20 each. A 'small Musadora' and a 'Box from Thompsons Seasons' were also included in a large assortment of enamel miniatures that Birch sold to George Oakley of London in April 1825.

Figure 15 Enamel miniature on copper, depicting Musidora (4.7 × 4.0 cm), executed by William Russell Birch, c. 1810. Reproduced courtesy of the Pennsylvania Academy of the Fine Arts.

was not the first or only one that depicted Musidora, however, for a Musidora miniature by Thomas Day (who had already produced a Musidora in crayons for the Royal Academy exhibition of 1777) had been on display at the annual exhibition of the Royal Academy in London in 1783 (*1783 Catalogue*, p. 4).[19] In a marked alteration by transmediation, an understanding of the nude female body as inherently sexualized and indecorous, and of Damon's illicit act of observing Musidora as improper, was countered in America by an expansion of the Musidora story that concluded with the union of Damon and Musidora: they marry.[20] This marriage, as in René Louis de Girardin's rewriting of Thomson's tale in his story of Musidora and Hylas,[21] both served as an antidote to and neutralized

---

[19] By that date, Musidora had not yet been illustrated in any American edition of *The Seasons*. In Britain, only John Murray's 1778 edition had boasted an illustration of the tale by Hamilton.

[20] The *Massachusetts Magazine* for August 1792 (pp. 475–6) published a prose rendering of Thomson's tale that concludes with the lovers' marriage and was accompanied by the first American illustration of Damon and Musidora by Samuel Hill. This prose version of the story was reprinted by the *Impartial Herald*, 13 December 1793.

[21] The translation of Girardin story was included in the English translation of *De la Composition des Paysages* (1777), *An Essay on Landscape*, which was published by James Dodsley in 1783. Girardin's story also memorializes Musidora and Hylas's love through an inscription because,

the potential indelicacy of the male lover's presence at Musidora's bath. Adapting the Thomsonian text or its visual mediation so as to reduce any inference of immorality or transgressiveness in the poet's 'luscious episode'[22] formed part of an effort to promote a single-mindedly moral reading of Musidora as not only inoffensive and innocent but also a model of femininity.

In the context of the purchasers of Birch's Musidora miniatures being exclusively male, it is likely that these enamels were primarily produced as highly personal objects for male consumption. Since the nude was not being related in late eighteenth- and early nineteenth-century America to classical incarnations of ideal beauty but rather understood as modern and catering to unlicensed desire, American artists still largely highlighted the impropriety of the undressed woman in visual art. The nudity of the figure, in this regard, particularly invited the beholder to reflect on her modesty and physicality. As a result, such a miniature – in contrast to an enamel miniature of bathing women who form part of a larger setting, and not visible in the same zoomed-in fashion as Birch's Musidora – may therefore not have been an appropriate gift for a woman.[23] Indeed, inferences of Musidora's sexuality may have complicated Musidora's virtuous inscription via the Thomsonian text. As 'portals to culture and behaviors of the past' (Scarpaci, 2016, p. 1), identical images (and even the same objects) were highly context-dependent: they could signify differently in line with prevailing cultural and national norms of decorum and morality within which these iconic media were perceived, sold and consumed.

Unlike reader-viewers of Du Roveray's version of Hamilton's design, those viewing Birch's miniature encountered a nude young woman who had been deracinated from the narrative framework of Thomson's tale, which had, of course, included Damon. Birch's Musidora is no longer presented as a bather, since the artist's image does not include the water into which she had already dipped her left foot in Hamilton's design; instead, we only see Musidora's body from her knees upwards. As such, the very reason for her seeking the woodland 'retreat' to avoid the heat of the day is removed, requiring that a new raison d'être be devised for her: that is, she is now on display exclusively for the pleasure of the person viewing her. Shorter than in Hamilton's original design, Musidora's hair no longer covers and frames her left breast but transforms her breasts into the focal point of the image. She resembles the Venus de' Medici, although the warm colouring contrasts with the monochrome mode in which the

---

apparently, the 'memory of these faithful lovers is still engraved on a neighbouring oak' (Girardin, 1783, p. 55).

[22] *The Nic-Nac; or, Literary Cabinet*, 2 (1823–4), p. 147.

[23] Birch produced such a landscape miniature, which is held by the Victorian and Albert Museum, accession number: P.14–1920.

Venus was usually rendered. The medium of the miniature also differed from copies of the Venus realized in marble or plaster of Paris because erotic miniatures were not meant for public display.

As an object conveying intimacy and primarily intended for private consumption, the miniature zoomed in on the nude female figure, aligning it through its medium (and despite its subject) with miniatures featuring portraits of real-life individuals. The medium provided an 'alternative semblance of the real' (Rabb, 2019, p. 5) in which Musidora's eyes and body, as well as her imagined mobility, become agents in a spectacle that arouses interest of various kinds. In the process, Musidora – although a literary character – simulates an authentic woman in the way in which the figure at the centre of the enamel plays a part in a performance of body display in which she is endowed with agency projected towards the beholder.

The miniature allows the person holding the object and gazing at Musidora to participate in the economy of looking that Thomson and Hamilton had established in their versions of the scene. In Birch's adaptation of Hamilton's design, Musidora's blue eyes are directed to the right, not directly encountering the viewer's. She probably looks, as Thomson characterized her, 'with timid eye around / The banks surveying' (1300–1), a description that Hamilton did not render accurately in iconic terms. Birch appears to cast her as modest, a visual characterization not offered by Hamilton's Musidora, who faces the viewer's gaze, inviting rather than avoiding the attention she is being paid as she is contemplated by the beholder. But he also amplifies her body, and especially her breasts, in a Rubenesque manner, which thus emphasizes her voluptuousness.

The individual privately contemplating Musidora replaces Damon's gaze. Yet the physical medium not only requires ocular apprehension but also necessitates physical engagement: the small, portable medium encouraged a tactile, personal connection between the image and the beholder. In fact, its very size made unavoidable a close physical relationship between the object and the viewer to ensure that its details, especially Musidora's facial expression, could be seen and interpreted. In this respect, as Jennifer Van Horn has observed, 'Miniatures' smooth ... surfaces and chased gold covers activated owners' sensory pleasure as the small depictions were held up to blushing cheeks or clasped over beating hearts' (Van Horn, 2017, p. 172). Enhanced with Musidora's visualization, the experience of sensory response and pleasure through looking at, holding and touching the object complicates the centrality of 'the convergence of text and image' (Lopez Szwydky, 2020, p. 105) that Lissette Lopez Szwydky posits as a defining mechanism of 'transmedia storytelling' by expanding the means of meaning-making from a visual and (mnemonic) script literary experience to include those of material-emotive literacy.

Damon's lover is not merely a platform for projection of desire, however. She also appears through the viewer's recalling of elements of the textual history of Musidora – the extra-iconic world of the poem – to gain a life of her own. She comes to life through the animated manner in which she is made to appear lifelike. The sensuousness of Birch's Musidora is enhanced by the light flesh colour that the artist uses for her body and the warm reds that he applies to her suffused cheeks, lips and nipples; the translucent realization of the garment that she is holding, moreover, contrasts with its appearance in the monochrome engravings in which the fabric had seemed more substantial. Birch creates a new realism of the erotic that relies on the medium of the miniature, advancing a view of a well-known character from *The Seasons* being recognized as tangible and capable of accommodating projected desire.

Those consumers who could obtain a copy of Birch's coloured Musidora would have treasured the precious object, fetishizing it in the way that Damon does Musidora in Thomson's story when he 'risk[s] the soul-distracting view' (1313) of his denuded lover. Musidora's lifelike chromatic appearance con-trasted with the black-and-white scene of Hamilton's illustration, which – framed by the codex and the typographical text – allowed less easily the figure's extra-textual imagining. Hamilton's Musidora was thus transformed from a display object at the 1801 annual exhibition of the Royal Academy into a mechanically reproduced copy available to book-buying and book-consuming individuals who had accessed his illustration through Du Roveray's upmarket edition. She was, furthermore, recoded as part of her being transplanted into the medial associational framework of the enamel miniature, turning into an exclusive figure now being contemplated by a privileged viewer who controlled access to this personal object.

Moreover, Birch's adaptation of Musidora as unframed by text, in marked contrast to both Hamilton's painting and the Du Roveray engraving, made his rendering more ambiguous. This textual deracination and her removal from Hamilton's composition advanced a less accurate understanding of Musidora's moral character and the reason for her nudity. The miniature's focus on Musidora's disrobed body and on her eyes – eyes only slightly turned from the viewer but not sufficiently so as not to recognize being observed – presents her as a voluptuous, self-confident and nubile woman who caters to a 'lawless gaze' (1311). Given the size of Birch's enamel painting, the direction of her glance needs to be gleaned through close study, possibly even by magnifying features through an optical device, an approach of the nude Musidora that breaks down the boundary Thomson established between her and Damon. Through the close observation necessary to anatomize the young woman's facial expression, the spatial distance between subject of observation and observer that is central in the majority of visualizations of Musidora and Damon is changed into a proximity between object held and beheld within the miniature painting and the individual's gaze that Thomson does not allow in his narrative.

The manipulation of the poet's relational aesthetics – in both the American title page design and, more decidedly, Birch's miniature – has consequences for the meanings of the different versions of Hamilton's design. As part of these relational aesthetics, Damon, within the setting of the woodland 'retreat', approached his lover unseen, from behind; he could not, as a consequence (and in contrast to Thomson's text) see her breasts. Removing the figure of Damon results in a situation where the modesty by which Musidora had been characterized is turned potentially into its opposite. Birch's revision of Hamilton's design, involving a level of extended reflective-participatory visual focus, thus also represents an alteration of the ways in which Musidora was cast by Thomson (and Hamilton) in relation to Damon, and not on her own. In fact, Hamilton's assigning to Damon's lover the garment that she is lifting provided an effective visual barrier to Damon. It obscured Musidora's sensual body from Damon and therefore served as a device of modesty and a screen against intra-iconic viewing. By contrast, the use in Birch's miniature of the same garment foregrounds Musidora by making her stand out from the stylized dark background: it no longer, as in the title page illustration for the 1814 edition, infers a protective environment and a sense of privacy. Birch's altered scene opens up to the right of the nude figure, potentially admitting additional viewers: Musidora's erotic inscription is now unregulated by background framing, and the miniature thus challenges the Thomsonian characterization of her as 'shr[inking] from herself' (1317). Of course, it is now the viewer who, as part of the intimate handling of the miniature, invades her privacy.

The title-page image of Musidora for the 1814 edition offered a different version of Thomson's story from the one that Hamilton had introduced, and although her innocence and purity were stressed through Damon's removal from the plate, Musidora's meaning had not changed dramatically. The revision of the image approximated Musidora to a statue of Venus, the contemplation of which is void of the personal erotic connection that linked Damon to Musidora. Birch's enamel rendering of her presented an altogether different version of the young woman, however. Despite her being situated in a landscape, she is domesticated as part of the medium of the miniature. In the process, she is made to signify differently from Hamilton's painterly scene and its American iteration: contained by the portable medium of the miniature, she functions as part of the emotionally and erotically inscribed materiality of the object itself. Her representation can be viewed, desired, touched. Birch's animation of Musidora, through the colouring of her body and especially of her eyes, endows her with an agency of looking that generates the illusion of her responsiveness to the beholder's contemplative engagement with her image. The illusion of softness that occurs because of the enamel pigment melting in such a way that the clear-cut lines of the original intaglio engraving no longer appear striking bestows upon her an organicity that the darkness of the elaborate engraved scenes in both Du Roveray and the American editions did not possess. Thus, it is the medial elements of the shape and size of the miniature, the enamel, including its technological properties of melting during the firing process, and the colour that – all meaningful individually – work together to create a fundamentally new version of Musidora than that first introduced to reader-viewers of Hamilton's engraving.

In the remediation of Kauffman's print and Hamilton's engraved design, the adaptation of Damon – his being cast as a boy in the case of the Duesbury vase and his removal from Birch's miniature – resulted in a change of perspective and a rewriting of Thomson's relational aesthetics: in the former case, Damon is cast as the melancholy but passionate lover eagerly observing the scene in front of him; by contrast, in the latter Musidora's relational contextualization needs to be undertaken by the viewer, who may not infer Damon in the reinvention of the young woman's storyworld. I have demonstrated that in the case of the Duesbury vase, the revision of Kauffman's design was undertaken in the interest of muting the eroticism of the voyeurism presented – through not only the alteration of the design, including the visual reformulation of Damon's identity, but also the reinforcing meaning of the material, pseudo-classical symbolism of the vase. The transmediation of Kauffman's and Hamilton's designs not only entails the mobility of images, their application onto another medium and the recontextualization of the images' meaningfulness but also creates the convergence of the different meanings of the media, both representational and material-symbolic.

4 Palemon, Lavinia and Virtuous Love Exemplified: From Creamware Jugs to Derby Figurines

This section will examine multiple instances of the transmediation of a design by William Lawrenson: transferred to different media over the course of forty years, the design was recontextualized, repurposed and made to convey distinct meanings that signalled changed interpretations of Thomson's vignette of Palemon and Lavinia in 'Autumn' (1730). John Raphael Smith executed an engraved version of a painting that Lawrenson had produced of the tale, which James Birchall published as a print of the lovers (measuring 50.3 × 35.3 cm)[24] in November 1780. The visualization of the two lovers revisited a theme that

---

[24] The modeller, J. J. Spengler, was responsible for the design. See Jewitt (1878, II, p. 96).

Figure 16 Mezzotint depicting Palemon and Lavinia (50.2 × 35.7 cm), designed by William Lawrenson and engraved by John Raphael Smith, 1780. Collection Sandro Jung.

Lawrenson had previously centralized in a painting that he exhibited at the Royal Academy exhibition of 1780 entitled 'Portrait in the character of a hay-maker' (p. 7).[25] The print was issued as a mezzotint in two states, in mono-chrome and as a delicately hand-coloured version (Figure 16).[26] By the end of the century, the design had been adapted for transfer-printing on pitchers and mugs manufactured in Liverpool. In 1800, the design was reused again, but this time in America. In this version, it served as the frontispiece to *Hymen's Recruiting-Serjeant*, a humorous work promoting matrimony by the Reverend M. L. Weems, which was addressed 'To all the Singles, whether Masculines or Feminines, throughout the United States' (Weems, 1800, p. 4). In Britain,

[25] John Raphael Smith engraved this painting as 'A Lady at Haymaking' for Birchall in 1781.

[26] On this print, which exists in two formats, one a rectangular full-page print, the other an oval, see Jung (2015, pp. 133–4).

however, Lawrenson's design migrated to yet another ceramic medium, the Royal Crown Derby manufacture producing pairs of figurines of Palemon and Lavinia in 1820, some of which are ornately coloured and gilt. Another state of the design, lacking the tree behind the lovers, sold as a biscuit version, a plain white, unglazed object. In contrast to the painted Derby figure, the biscuit rendering invoked a miniaturized version of statuary in marble or plaster of Paris. Once again, we see an object that, through its materiality, creates an association with the classical past and neoclassical fashions that transform the figures into proto-mythological characters.

Each of the different transmedially used versions of Lawrenson's visualization of Thomson's lovers offered iterations of the tale that, at times, eliminated ambiguities of the poet's characterization; at other times, it recontextualized them in terms of class difference. At yet other times, Palemon and Lavinia were made to serve as placeholders for real-life personages whom Thomson did not know at the time when he produced his vignette. The poet's vignette focused on the 'discovery' of Lavinia, the daughter of the once wealthy Acasto, who after her father's death and financial ruin retires with her mother to a rural community where her formerly high social status is not known. In this environment, she is obliged to glean the fields to subsist, in the process becoming associated with the working-class labourers who harvest the crop on behalf of their master. She is encountered carrying out this activity by the landowner, Palemon, who used to partake of Acasto's beneficence and recognizes not only Lavinia's unrivalled beauty but also her innate worth. Not before Palemon has vanquished his class-specific prejudices and learned of Lavinia's origin as his former benefactor's daughter, however, can he declare his love to the gleaner and propose marriage to her. Lawrenson's visual capturing of the lovers' story recasts Lavinia in a way that distinguishes her starkly from her social inferiors: in effect, his composition makes both Lavinia and Palemon appear as social equals. His version of Lavinia clearly did not accurately reflect Thomson's story: he introduces visual cues involving the individuals in the background and the specific setting of the scene that obscure the moment of discovery and the acknowledgement of Lavinia's originary class status; he emphasizes her nobility and – evidenced through dress conventions – her fashionable sophistication. Hence, Lawrenson's visual interpretation of Thomson's tale advanced a one-sided understanding of Lavinia that stresses her union with Palemon at the cost of relating her family's misfortune and her struggling as an indigent gleaner. Yet this struggle, as well as her caring for her aged mother, was central to Thomson's characterization of Lavinia as morally noble. In this respect, Lawrenson's choice of Lavinia as a lover (rather than as the daughter of Acasto) whose poverty remains unacknowledged offers a more romanticized version of Thomson's gleaner. Lawrenson's composition authorizes no hesitation on Palemon's part regarding whether or not he could love the young woman.

Different technologies to reproduce illustrations, including copper engraving, transfer-printing and the moulding of clay and other ceramic substrates, facilitated the wide-ranging adoption of Lawrenson's design. This section will argue that these text technologies specifically facilitated the reproduction of the illustration, incorporating it within the material framework of objects that depended for their intermedial meanings on the material-literary-symbolic literacy of buyers and viewers of these productions. Importantly, in the process of Lawrenson's visualization becoming an integral part of the substrate carrying or embodying it, the producers of these visually enhanced objects also adapted the design. In terms of interpretation and meaning, we cannot ignore that, while announcing through the use of Palemon and Lavinia's names 'an overt and defining relationship to [a] prior text', they also 'transcod[ed]' the vignette (Hutcheon, 2012, p. 3, p. 7). This 'transcoding' entailed a process of 'repetition with variation' (Hutcheon, 2012, p. 4) whereby the illustration is *largely* copied accurately, but meaningful visual alteration is introduced (such as the omission of characters, objects and settings, as well as the redefinition of intra-iconic relationships between characters). Focusing on instances of iconic revision, I will argue that in the process of engaging with Thomson's story, manufacturers of literary material culture identified potential moral ambiguities in the tale or features in Lawrenson's design that established associations with real-life individuals, which they then suppressed by either altering the design or eliminating these iconic features altogether. Transmediation, in this respect, also involved a particular reinterpretation of the vignette, new relational meanings being constructed both intra-iconically and intermedially. Significantly, intermedial meanings encouraged different interpretation precisely because these objects functioned as part of different social practices.

As this section will demonstrate, Birchall's print of Lawrenson's painting, which retailed at seven and a half shillings and was issued at the start of the vogue for visual renderings of Palemon and Lavinia, enjoyed a life beyond its connection with Thomson's lovers. It evoked esoteric stories only accessible to those readers who recognized the particular setting depicted as 'the palpable presence of actuality in the Jacobean house in the background' (D'Oench, 1999, p. 88). Birchall's engraving appears to have been the first furniture print to be produced of the lovers and was published as part of a pair, its companion being an engraving of Lawrenson's painting of Cymon and Iphigenia, also engraved by Smith (Frankau, 1902, p. 188). In addition to paintings exhibited at the Royal Academy between 1784 and 1798, including Sophia Howell's 'The Discovery of Lavinia', William Beechy's 'Lavinia returned from Gleaning', a subject that S. Medley also selected, and Samuel Shelley's 'Lavinia and her Mother', several prints issued between 1782 and 1785 depicted the courtship scene featuring Palemon and Lavinia, Lavinia and her mother, or Lavinia on her own. None of these prints experienced as medially diverse an afterlife as Lawrenson's rendering, however.

The different prints depicting Palemon and Lavinia contributed to a larger cultural phenomenon that generated a wide-ranging material and literary after-life of the Thomsonian lovers. 'The Story of Lavinia' routinely featured in the 'moral' rubric of miscellanies of poems, including Oliver Goldsmith's 1770 anthology, *Poems for young Ladies*, 'devotional, moral, and entertaining'. The popularity of the story and its characters at the start of the 1780s can be gleaned by a notice of a masquerade at which 'Mrs Blackburn in Lavinia [had] looked divinely; everyone wished to be a Palemon'.[27] Glossing of the names was not necessary because of the multifarious ways in which individuals since the late 1770s could have become acquainted with the tale: from public readings and lectures on elocution by 'Mr Cresswick' at the Old Theatre in Portugal Street in October 1779 to 'a very pretty Pastoral Ballet' called 'Palemon and Lavinia' whose run started from February 1782.[28] Thomson's vignette was variously performed, transforming into a spectacular enactment of the work's sentimental class politics. It was revisited by other authors keen to produce different versions of the story: imaginative expansions such as David Mountfort's *Palemon and Lavinia: A legendary Tale … Enlarged from a Story in Thomson's Seasons* (1783) or rewritings of the tale that, as in the poem, 'Palemon and Lavinia', cast Lavinia as a 'cruel charmer'.[29] The characters were also frequently invoked in love poems, at times even referenced in the poem title, as in William Crowe's 'To a young Gentlewoman, with Thomson's Seasons, doubled down at the Story of Palemon and Lavinia' (1804).

From 1778 the tale, which was frequently read as Thomson's version of the biblical Ruth and Boaz story, had already served as the subject for book illustrations; it was also adopted as part of motifs selected by women for their embroidery work, including the rare transmedial use in the medium of needle-work on silk of an existing book illustration of the lovers that had been included in J. Strachan and W. Stewart's 1792 London edition of *The Seasons*.[30] These various iterations of the tale promoted widespread familiarity with Thomson's story and helped readers to imagine the two lovers; in turn, the visual

---

27 *Parker's General Advertiser*, 19 September 1782.
28 *Morning Post and Daily Advertiser*, 28 October 1779; *Public Advertiser*, 22 February 1782.
29 'Palemon and Lavinia', *The European Magazine*, 48 (1805), p. 306.
30 The needlework picture of Palemon and Lavinia sold at Sotheby's on 25 June 2001. While the embroidered image generally accurately copies Charles Ansell's illustration, it omits the figure of the reaper in the right-hand middle ground.

concretizations produced from the 1780s onwards inspired producers of fashionable material culture to represent the story as part of the objects that they manufactured, for they recognized that the desire advanced by the two lovers transformed them into desirable commodities. They represented a version of romance that could be appropriately framed in the interiors of the well-to-do where the story – in contrast to the original tale of labour – invoked associations of pastoral alongside those of courtship and love.

Lawrenson's composition represents a staged and stylized scene in which Lavinia's nobility is highlighted: similar to Samuel Richardson's Pamela in her country dress and to the subject of Lawrenson's 'A Lady at Haymaking', Lavinia appears to be playing a part in a refined scene of courtship. Now, though, she impersonates Thomson's character in appropriate costume, which, as noted earlier, was by 1782 available for use at masquerades. For the readers of the 1781 number of *Neue Bibliothek der schönen Wissenschaften und freyen Künste*, the print's subject was glossed as depicting two discrete moments from Thomson's tale: the discovery of Lavinia while gleaning, as well as the ensuing declaration of love from Palemon.[31] At the same time and beyond this gloss, the meaning of the print was not definite or definitive. Instead, it possessed an esoteric meaning that has been obscured over time in much the same way that the material-textual inscription of the Derby figurines as remediations of Lawrenson's design requires re-activation in order to understand their popular cultural value as iconic representations of Thomson's two lovers. Smith's engraving was captioned 'Palemon & Lavinia. See Thompson's Autumn'. The named fictional characters were embedded within a scene that featured on the right an accurate reproduction of Holland House in Kensington. Fiction met real life. Even though this stately home was not mentioned by the poet, the addition of this identifiable architectural structure underscored the realism of the scene depicted and an anchoring mechanism for Thomson's tale. At the same time, to viewers with sufficient visual and cultural literacy, the rendering of Holland House served as a cue to understanding Palemon and Lavinia as placeholders for individuals with a particular connection to Holland House, the residence of Henry Fox, first Baron Holland and, among other public offices he held, secretary of state under the Duke of Newcastle.

We should not underestimate the complexity of the transmedial process here. Stephen Bending has noted that Lawrenson's design of the two lovers was 'popularly thought to represent George III and Lady Sarah Lennox' (Bending, 2013, p. 2), the woman to whom the King contemplated making an offer of marriage. According to Horace Walpole, Lady Sarah had, in her youth, played

---

[31] *Neue Bibliothek der schönen Wissenschaften und freyen Künste*, 26 (1781), p. 360.

the part of haymaker in the fields of Holland Park (Napier, 1901, I, p. 49 n.). It is thus her role play and the King's amorous sentiments at the time she arrived at court in 1760 that Lawrenson represents in terms of two literary characters' courtship. The group of lovers, the woman a gleaner, the male figure a wealthy landowner, thus was imbued with popular-cultural meanings that went beyond Thomson's story.

Indeed, we see the potential polysemy of the depiction further strengthened through the symbolic language of dress, for Lavinia's apron possesses an ambiguity that related her to both servant figures and the fashionable adoption and public display of the apron as a garment worn by elite women (Spencer, 2018, p. 168). Even though the apron had traditionally been 'associated . . . with labouring women', 'ladies imitating their inferiors by wearing aprons' (Spencer, 2018, p. 165) sought to evoke associations with rustic simplicity and innocence. Elizabeth Spencer suggests that the apron-wearing Lavinia not only served as an emblem of rural innocence but that she also represented the 'robust fertility' of country girls – Lavinia, as she gathers the harvest in her apron, 'aligning herself with the fertility and reproductive cycle of the land' (Spencer, 2018, p. 169). More to the point, despite Thomson's characterization of Lavinia as chaste and innocent, the manner of her visualization and the role of the apron as a feature of her acting a part rewrite the way in which the poet had cast her. The storyworld of the print thus potentially encouraged two courtship narratives rather than one: the one anchored in Thomson's text, the other alluding to the king's known passion for Lady Sarah, including the known connection that the latter had to Holland House, her sister's residence, where Lady Sarah had lived since the age of thirteen. These latter, extra-textual associations complicated Lavinia's story and characterization. For, those readers with knowledge of Lady Sarah's story could infer meanings that were not part of the Palemon and Lavinia tale and in the process transform the story into a masked version of King George's courtship of Lady Sarah.

Even without knowledge of the possible identification of Palemon and Lavinia with George III and Lady Sarah and the fact that the King was dissuaded from marrying her by his advisers (as well as by her subsequent notoriety, including an elopement and divorce), the scene of courtship as represented raised questions of morality and decorum that were subsequently addressed in the transmediation of the design. By the time that Birchall issued the print in 1780, the story involving the King and Lady Sarah was twenty years old. Even so, it may still have resonated in terms of a nostalgic version of romance, invigorating a memory that captured both figures at a moment in time that preceded Palemon and Lavinia's nuptials but did not culminate in Lady Sarah's union with George III.

How pervasively iconic Lawrenson's rendering of Palemon and Lavinia was and to what degree it stimulated associations beyond Thomson's story cannot, of course, be determined. But the fact that alterations to the design of the print retailed by Birchall were made when it was transmediated indicates that issues of morality were at stake and that in the three-dimensional realization of the characters, the elimination of Holland House removed any associative link that viewers might have established with George III and Lady Sarah. In the remainder of this section, I shall examine the appropriation of Lawrenson's design for application on different media in order to determine which new meanings the alterations of the design generated.

Late eighteenth-century manufacturers of creamware jugs and mugs adopted Lawrenson's design as part of the embellishment of their wares. Creamware was a refined earthenware that had been developed in the mid-eighteenth century as a more affordable alternative to porcelain. Its producers, and specialist makers at Liverpool in particular, deployed the new technology of transfer-printing developed in the 1760s to copy existing designs and apply them to their wares for domestic use. Thus, these iconically enhanced objects could also fulfil a decorative and literacy-enhancing display function. The transfer-printed illustrations pointed to the objects' 'primary intended function' as 'display elements on dressers' rather than their 'primary intended use' as containers of food items (Brooks, 2010, p. 158, p. 160). According to Gavin Lucas, they also fulfilled an identity-formational purpose, reflecting particular choices of transfer-printed subjects that correlated to cultural aspirations; and these choices informed engagement with the ideological inscription of the texts now made palatable to user-readers through the medium of tableware (Lucas, 2003, p. 128).

The jugs and mugs that featured an adapted version of Lawrenson's design formed part of a group of creamware objects that occupied the lower end of the spectrum of this kind of pottery, the upper end being represented by ornately glazed and moulded items, including hand-painted and polychrome-glazed tea pots. The transfer-printing of illustrations constituted a text technology that facilitated the production of large numbers of ceramics featuring identical illustrations and transformed plain tableware into particularized objects of contemplation. With the lovers' names given underneath the image, these illustrated objects served as access nodes to cultural meanings that would be directed and fed by Lawrenson's design. The featuring on the ceramic objects of 'Palemon and Lavinia' initiated what Julie Sanders, writing about intertextuality and adaptation, comprehends in terms of 'the performance of echo and allusion' (Sanders, 2016, p. 4). These poetical names invoke a textual realm beyond that of the jug and mug, inviting reader-viewers to make connections with Thomson's story.

The transmedial use of Lawrenson's design necessarily entailed a resizing of the illustration, but it also encouraged a new medial relationship with an image of a pastoral setting that was printed on the reverse of the jug. Relational meaning-making practices had already been at work in the set of prints made up of Lawrenson's two companion pieces for Birchall: the eroticized scene from Boccaccio's *Decameron* (and especially Iphigenia's bared breast) jarring with (or reinscribing) the sentimental scene of Thomson's lovers. Whereas the distinct medial entities of the two prints encouraged one type of interpretation, the surface of the jug served as a physical contact zone for the two illustrations. As such, it could facilitate an associative connection between the two images that neither of the illustrations as separate prints would have generated. Beyond the size and surface requirements of the creamware medium, moreover, the manufacturers of the jug altered the artist's design. Altering details that related to the figures in the background had ramifications for the interpretation of the scene as an idyllic enactment of romantic courtship: in the transfer-printed version the figures in the background look at one another, rather than in the direction of Palemon and Lavinia. In keeping with a general move towards class obfuscation, these figures are no longer to be clearly identified as labourers because they no longer hold the sickles with which Lawrenson had equipped them.

While the use of complex designs for transfer-printing on ceramic objects often entailed a process of reducing and simplifying background detail, as well as highlighting a central scene at the cost of additional, secondary areas of the illustrations beyond the centre, the reorientation of the harvesters' gaze signified the rewriting of Lawrenson's visual narrative. For in Birchall's print, the harvesters had served the chaperone function of witnessing both Lavinia's modesty and Palemon's approach; and it is their presence in the image, facing as they do the viewer rather than their actually being able to see the two lovers (who are partially concealed from them by the tree in front of which they are standing), that impresses their importance on the viewer. Birchall's version of the labourers had relied on the iconographic conventions that Lawrenson had encoded to designate these figures as georgic agents, so the changing of the design for transfer-printed objects also entailed an act of generic re-inscription and reorientation from georgic to pastoral. The adaptation of Lawrenson's image for use on ceramics thus reflected 'a process involving the transition from one genre to another' (Sanders, 2016, p. 20), including a shifting of emphasis from the moment of 'discovery' to the lovers' union.

In the majority of eighteenth-century illustrations of the Palemon and Lavinia tale, the harvesters had validated Palemon's declaration of love as public; thus, they countered the ambiguous erotic inscription of his gaze and contemplation of Lavinia's bodily attractiveness (Jung, 2015, p. 131). Lawrenson had introduced the harvester figures, who do not feature as observers of the scene in the original tale, for a particular reason. He needed to provide an unambiguous storyworld. But Thomson's own account of Palemon's reaction on encountering Lavinia was ambiguous: it stressed both his 'love and chaste desire' (231) and his 'mingled passions' (256); as well, it included the landowner's confronting his own prejudices regarding the possibility of social mobility. Fantasizing that because of her low station Lavinia must be destined for 'the rude embrace / Of some indecent clown' (240–1), Palemon is conflicted about what is due to his superior social position. At the same time, he ponders how societal prejudices can be reconciled with his personal feelings for Lavinia. These reflections are triggered by her physical beauty, for she was 'beauty's self' (207), rather than by any selfless wish to assist the indigent young woman, an aspect of Palemon's 'discovery' of Lavinia that one critic considered contrived and 'too artificial'.[32] Visual artists' introduction of the harvesters thus entailed the labourers' instrumentalization for the specific end of shaping the tale's reception; especially, it directed the reading process so that the harvesters serve as public observers of a morally unobjectionable encounter between Palemon and Lavinia. Such artistic intervention clarified meaning at the same time as it eliminated possible other readings. For Thomson's characterization of Lavinia as an embodiment of 'bashful modesty' (185), 'unstain'd, and pure' (193), on the one hand, and Palemon's desire-infused recognition of her striking beauty, on the other, allowed potentially conflicting readings because it remains unclear whether or not Lavinia's bodily attractiveness or her modesty induced Palemon's declaration of love. It would seem the artists concluded that in order to direct the reader's understanding of Palemon's recognition of Lavinia's virtue as responsible for his love, the landowner's erotic fantasy needed to be muted through a witnessed public enactment of his respectful courtship.

Lawrenson's design therefore offered a guided reading in which Palemon and Lavinia appear in a courtship scene that does not deliberately infer or represent the ambiguity of Palemon's motivation to elevate Lavinia from the station of a gleaner. Artists' introduction of the harvesters aligned Lavinia with the labourers through their common activity on the field but also distinguished her from them: 'her polish'd limbs' (202) contrasted with the 'rude[ness]' that Palemon associates with labourers. In Smith's realization of Lawrenson's design, in marked distinction from any other illustration of the tale, the harvesters are standing in the background rather than working. Their sightline establishes a connection with both Lavinia and Palemon that relates to their existing knowledge concerning Lavinia's want but also regarding the social position of

---

[32] 'Critical Remarks on the Poetry of Thomson', *Scots Magazine*, 1 November 1795, p. 708.

Palemon as their master. Their gaze appears to be one of interest (whereas the two figures in the background of Birchall's print do not engage with one another but are engaged in an act of observation), which the viewer may interpret as their probing of the precise meaning of the courtship scene taking place in the foreground. The fact that Lawrenson's design of the two labourers was altered for use on transfer-printed wares assigns particular importance to them. Redirecting their gaze removes their attention from Palemon and Lavinia and redefines their role in the design.

According to Thomson, Palemon's 'discovery' of Lavinia represented a courtship scene between two individuals who are not each other's equals. Lawrenson, as we saw, obscures this social difference through Lavinia's elegant clothing. Even so, once artisans adopted Lawrenson's illustration for use on creamware objects, the dramatization of the meeting of two classes became potentially problematic, at least to those reader-viewers able to identify the extent of the adaptation of Thomson's original class-defined relationship between Palemon and Lavinia. For the consumers of these objects, Lavinia's class affiliation needed to be differentiated from the harvesters by denying that she (even temporarily) shared their condition even if she was now removed from them. The reorientation of the gaze of Lawrenson's gleaners and the removal of their emblems of work, the sickles, facilitated a reductive rendering of the story that no longer problematized Lavinia's unprotected status and ambiguous class-defined identity. The harvesters' not paying attention to the lovers removes the connection and alignment between them and Lavinia introduced by Lawrenson. It thus signals the resolution of the gleaner's plight: she is not only distant from the field labourers in terms of her upbringing and sophistication but is also completely removed from their sphere through her elevation as Palemon's future wife.

Significantly, then, since the pitcher was a ceramic object to be used in the household, the illustration of the two lovers would have been viewed frequently and functioned as an expressive medium of upper-class sentimental politics. It visualized Thomson's famed lovers without raising Lavinia's initially ambiguous class identity by invoking or inferring it through cues in the image (Figure 17). Because the spatial distance between the group at the back and Palemon and Lavinia at the front reinforced their social separation, it also implied that Lavinia's fate – the recognition of her worth and subsequent elevation – fell far beyond the labourers' reach. Lavinia's elevation did not, as such, assert an instance of upward mobility but enforced a reclaiming of an individual from Palemon's class. Rather than mere onlookers, moreover, the harvesters on the pitcher function as romantic agents themselves. In this version of Lawrenson's design, the two harvesters are cast as lovers, the male figure

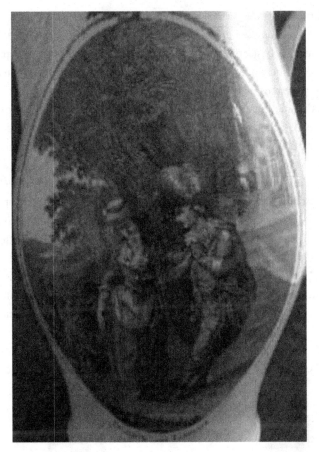

Figure 17 Transfer-printed jug featuring Palemon and Lavinia (height: 16 cm).
Collection Sandro Jung.

putting his arm around the woman and the group of harvesters mirroring in the background the scene that is enacted by Palemon and Lavinia. The design on the pitcher emphasizes their commonality rather than their social difference, bringing them together in a way that Thomson's tale did not. As such, it illustrates the possibility of romantic love for all classes.

In another respect, the transfer-printed iterations of Lawrenson's design on pitchers differed from Birchall's print. Both Palemon and Lavinia appear to be fashionably dressed, the master's plumed hat being a particularly striking accessory. Palemon is cast as Lavinia's social superior in the print, although the details of both figures' clothing reflect their socially elevated status, the coloured version of the mezzotint even revealing a fine pattern on her shawl as well as the delicacy of her face and luxuriant hair. By contrast, no such details are discernible in the transfer-printed image, where the materiality of Lavinia's dress fabric appears coarser and the fineness of her facial portrait is not conveyed. Whereas Lawrenson had rendered her as a highly stylized portrayal of a gleaner, the cost-effective transfer-printing is not capable of reproducing the tonal sophistication of the (coloured) mezzotint because of its focus on line; accordingly, it presents a less refined version of Lavinia that aligns her with the harvesters' 'rude' character. The realization of Lavinia on the jug centres on representing her character as a gleaner rather than on depicting her with the level of sophistication with which Smith had rendered her in the mezzotint.

In addition to the design on the jug discussed, another version of Lawrenson's design was used for transfer-printing on jugs and mugs (Drakard, 1992, p. 64). The latter adaptation retains the two reapers in the background, except that they are looking at one another rather than towards Palemon and Lavinia (Figure 18). The ears of corn that Lavinia carries are barely distinguishable from the foliage of the tree, which effectively lessens the association between her and the act of gleaning. Her face is rendered more delicately, the reduced tonality of the print putting into sharper relief the figure design. The most radical change introduced in this version of Lawrenson's design is the replacement of Holland House: now, we see a non-identifiable mansion much further in the background than Palemon's home had been in the print and the transmediated version of the jug discussed earlier. The physical distance between the mansion and Palemon also

Figure 18 Transfer-printed jug featuring Palemon and Lavinia (height: 16.2 cm). Collection Sandro Jung.

removes the strong association between the two that Lawrenson had emphasized, especially once the two horses held by the groom in front of Holland
House in Lawrenson's print and their potential connection with the two lovers
are considered. For these horses without riders could be related to Palemon and
Lavinia (or the King and Lady Sarah) who, after horse riding, may have gone for
a walk, during which the latter assumed the role of gleaner. These visual devices
allow an imaginative expansion of the Thomsonian story not afforded by the
removal of Holland House and the horses. Whereas the introduction of Holland
House would have provided an iconic cue to allow an identification of Lavinia
with Lady Sarah, this identification in the absence of the specific architectural
location is no longer possible.

   Similar to the replacement of the architectural feat represented on the second
jug, the revision of Lawrenson's design for use as the copper-engraved frontispiece of Weems's *Hymen's Recruiting-Serjeant* concerned Holland House
(Figure 19). In the case of the American publication, the mansion was removed
altogether and the space that it had previously occupied was transformed into
a field. To the readers of Weems' pamphlet, which focused on the subject of

Figure 19 Copper-engraved cover vignette, *Hymen's Recruiting-Serjeant*
(Philadelphia: M. L. Weems, 1800). Courtesy of the Maryland Center for
History and Culture.

matrimony in an especially national, American (as opposed to a British) context, the visual reference to a foreign site that carried aristocratic associations, including those reminders of former American dependence on Britain that Weems rejected in his publication, would have been out of place. For at that time, American visual culture increasingly turned to the representation of indigenous landscapes and national architecture. Furthermore, while the identification in Britain of Palemon and Lavinia in relation to Holland House may have evoked the story of Lady Sarah and the King, by 1800, American reader-viewers, without proper visual cues and unsupported by anecdotal references such as Walpole's, would likely not have been able to recover the non-Thomsonian story. Weems did not promote sentimental politics; the frontispiece nevertheless furnished the names of Thomson's lovers, including the lines of poetry that had originally featured on Birchall's print, a reproduction process that fixed their meaning, rather than allowing an alternative identification.

Whereas the jugs, mugs and Weems's frontispiece featuring Lawrenson's design would have relied respectively on the reproductive technologies of transfer-printing and copper engraving to create objects that were identical in appearance, no such focus on uniformity can be identified in the appropriation of the design by the Derby porcelain manufacture. Not only were the Derby figurines expensive upmarket display objects that invoked associations of precious text-technological substrates such as marble or substances such as expensive pigment, these objects also drew attention to their symbolic inscription with particular economic value (Figure 20). The non-biscuit versions were, furthermore, characterized by their individual colour schemes. In this respect, the figurines certainly were the result of reproductive processes facilitated by a mould but subsequently transformed through the application of colour into unique items inferring artistic aura. The origin of the figurine in Lawrenson's print has not hitherto been recognized and has been obscured – in terms of both the three-dimensional realization of the group and the striking colouring of the figures – through the fundamental medial difference from the print (Figure 21).

In yet another respect, the figurines were deracinated from the original context of Lawrenson's print: both the mansion and the gleaners in the right- and left-hand background respectively are removed. This omission of contextual elements that convey the triangular connectedness between Lavinia, the reapers and Palemon reduces the ability of the figurine to trigger recall of the story of the lovers beyond their union – a moment that in poetic captions to prints had usually been glossed as either Palemon's 'discovery' of Lavinia or his declaration of love to her. If the three-line poetry caption to Birchall's print emphasized Lavinia's (indirect) agency – 'Won by the Charm / Of goodness irresistible, and all / In sweet disorder lost, she blushd consent' – the cost of Lavinia's social

Figure 20 Derby biscuit figurine of Palemon and Lavinia (height: 27.5 cm), c. 1790. Collection Sandro Jung.

transformation is thus her voiceless acquiescence to Palemon's courtship, an agency that removes her from the active sphere of gleaning to the silent language of looks and blushes. In contrast to the print and the design on the pitcher, the expensive materiality of the Derby object obscures the young woman's sudden elevation and removal from poverty. The gilding on cobalt-blue, which is used for Lavinia's dress and Palemon's waistcoat, as well as the gilt stripes on the latter's pantaloons, reveal these figurines to be luxury objects for display: utilizing colours ranging from blue to pink, they underscore the characters' symbolic nobility.[33] The range of detail in the figures themselves (the floral painting on Lavinia's upper garment, the ribbons and bow, as well as the finely executed foliage) and colour palette applied speak to the exceptional material quality of this transmedial iteration of Lawrenson's two-dimensional design. The details of Lavinia's clothing instance the kind of fashionable dress that may have been worn by women who were either impersonating the character on a particular occasion or painted, as was Frances Talbot, 'in the character of Lavinia' (*1802 Catalogue*, p. 14).[34] Migrating across media from print to ceramics, Lawrenson's design in

---

[33] These comments on the colouring and decoration of the figurine are based on the copy at the Royal Crown Derby Museum. A copy with distinctly different colouring sold at Paul Beighton Auctioneers Ltd in March 2020.

[34] John Opie exhibited his painting at the Royal Academy in 1802.

Figure 21 Painted Royal Crown Derby figurine of Palemon and Lavinia (height: 33 cm), 1820. Courtesy the Royal Crown Derby Museum Charitable Trust.

its presentation of dress not only appropriated existing fashions but in turn may have inspired particular fashionings of Lavinia in real life.

Each medium transforms and adapts a transmedially used design by endowing it with associations of its material properties and imagined or inferred uses. In the case of William Lawrenson's design of Thomson's Palemon and Lavinia, the image not only possessed an intertextual connection with *The Seasons* but was also associated with King George III's courtship of Lady Sarah Lennox, the poet's lovers serving as pastoral placeholders. It gained extra-textual meaning for those consumers able to purchase the engraved version of Lawrenson's design, who were thus able not only to take part in the literary material culture of the day but also to share in the esoteric culture of occasion that was frequently exploited by producers of literary material culture. Lawrenson's visualization of the Palemon and Lavinia tale, in this respect, did more than merely select what was to become an iconic courtship scene and that would be replicated by numerous artists. When his design was adapted for use on a medium that was marketed among a much broader range of purchasers of ceramic wares for day-to-day use, transmediation not only changed the relationship that the gleaners entertained with the reapers but also altered the function that Lawrenson had assigned to the latter as chaperones. No longer framed as the print had been or monumentalized in a portfolio, the jug and mug were part of a framework of domestic use that may have included their being contemplated but also their being utilized. In the process, they introduced the sentimental politics of Thomson's tale as mediated by the adaptor of the image for the creamware objects to their beholders.

Lawrenson had already rewritten Thomson's story by directing an interpretation that would omit the moral ambiguity of the poet's story. The visual constellation he created between the gleaners and Lavinia was, in turn, visually rewritten because the design was adapted for use on transfer-printed wares. By 1800, the visual reference to British architecture, Holland House, disappeared to promote not only Weems's advocacy of matrimony among Americans but also the symbolic associations that the edifice possessed with Britain's past and stories with which American readers may not have been familiar. When Lawrenson's design was translated again into a three-dimensional figurine, his Palemon and Lavinia no longer appeared in a landscape dominated by Holland House, and the observant harvesters were removed as well. The Derby Palemon and Lavinia figures could no longer be mistaken for the indigent Lavinia before her discovery and a Palemon reticent to declare his passion for her. Sold as Palemon and Lavinia, the figurines served as the embodiments of sentimental love but, without the mechanisms deliberately introduced in the planar media to demarcate different classes, emphasize morality or create a scene in which the lovers at the front of the design are mirrored by those figures at the back. The reception of the Palemon and Lavinia story, studied through the lens of Lawrenson's design and its transmedial applications, is characterized by a complex engagement on the part of agents – visual readers and commercial producers of commodity products – who changed, adapted and rewrote Thomson's text for their own ends. These changes were subtle and often ideological, but readers, as the different text-technological engagements with Thomson's tale evidence, were attuned to encountering and making sense of adaptations. The elevation of Lavinia was, according to Abigail Williams, 'an antimaterialistic moment vigorously marketed as a saleable commodity' (Williams, 2017, p. 154). Accordingly, the means to create ever new embodiments of and engagements with the tale lay in the reproductive text technologies of the time and its being harnessed by the producers of fashionable literary material culture. These text technologies facilitated an interpretation of Thomson's vignette that no longer highlighted the didactic-moralizing agenda of both the tale and the poem from which the former was frequently excerpted. Privileging the anthropocentric focus of the tale, Lawrenson and those adapting his visualization transmedially indirectly redefined the sentimental-instructive import of the story. At the same time, they also replaced the predominant generic modes of Thomson's tale – the georgic and the pathetic – with those of the amatory and even the sensational, the latter especially if Palemon and Lavinia were identified with the King and Lady Sarah.

5 Re-narrating *Robinson Crusoe*: Transmediation on French Speaking Plates

This section will discuss the transmediation of English and French book illustrations on two sets of French 'speaking plates', *assiettes parlantes*, that were produced between the 1820s and the 1850s. Moving away from the single-illustration focus of the earlier sections of this Element, I will argue that once entire sets of literary illustrations of *Robinson Crusoe* were transmediated onto a group of identical medial forms, the predefined inter-iconic connectedness that underpinned these visualizations as book illustrations with clear referential connections with the printed text became tenuous. Through transmediation, the series defined by the sequentiality of the illustrations and their meaningful placement within the codex transforms into a more fluid grouping of visualizations that then operates according to the modal properties of the object onto which they are printed.

I will examine the transmediation of two sets of book illustrations of *Robinson Crusoe* by Thomas Stothard and J. J. Grandville on French *assiettes parlantes*. These plates were produced by the Montereau and Creil-Montereau manufactures respectively. My account will chart how the materiality and mediality of the plates shaped meaning and directed reading/viewing experience. Focusing on the processes that altered the artists' visualizations, including how perspective, emphases and details were changed, it will probe the hybrid make-up of these image-texts as composed of images and writing and, in particular, how the captions to the illustrations in the English and French editions and the French plates facilitated the viewers' meaning-making. In addition, this section will study how these intermedial constellations generate meanings that extend those of the illustrated codex while redefining the textual dynamics of the storyworlds they depict in the physical framework of the transfer-printed plates.

At the start of the nineteenth century, French adaptations of Stothard's series of illustrations for John Stockdale's 1790 London edition appeared. In three editions of translations of Defoe's novel, and especially on a set of twelve plates produced by the Montereau ceramic manufacture, these adaptations not only introduced to viewers of these images a changed modality and new presentational manner. But they also created illustrations on the ceramic plates that signalled a new use of these visual texts that relied on readers' mnemonic ability to recreate contextual frameworks through inference and recall. Part of this process of reading the illustrations on the speaking plates involved the short text caption in the cartouche below the printed image, which furnished a gateway that invited textual recovery or imaginative expansion or a mixture of both. The transplanting of Stothard's images from the paper-based medium of the edition onto the well or interior surface of the plate entailed a process of 'transformational transmission' (Taylor, 2009, p. 95) that removed them from the physically contained storyworld of the illustrated edition. They were recontextualized as part of a world of use into one where the spatio-temporal characteristics of their originary storyworld were redefined through the medial mobility and detachability of individual plates from the set, featuring different scenes from Stothard's series. As 'intertextual filters through which prior versions must be "read"' (Meyers, McKnight and Krabbenhoft, 2014, p. 100), the transmedially used illustrations reveal intra-textual connections that encouraged readers to relate characters and agency, as well as settings. At the same time, both the visual modality of the engraved image and the materiality of the ceramic plates shaped the experience of the wider extra-textually imagined storyworld, which of course cannot be separated from the social occasion on which these ceramic objects are used. This complexity of experience occurs because 'each medium in a transmedia narrative contributes a unique aspect of the story, drawing on the strength of the particular format, often providing multiple points of entry for audiences' (Meyers, McKnight and Krabbenhoft, 2014, p. 98). The multi-modal make-up of the plates, including the cartouche-image hybrid on the ceramic substrate, allows a reading of the literary materiality of these tableware items conditioned as much by the material-textual literacy of the beholder as by the cultural resonance of Stothard's illustrations at the time.

The use of Stothard's designs on the plates transformed these tableware items into literary display objects that operated within an economy of reading and apprehension fundamentally different from the designs' original functioning as book illustrations. Typically, adapting the rectangular designs in portrait orientation to the circular format of the well of the plate repeatedly involved the omission of background detail. Such detail had offered reader-viewers of Stothard's designs clues to the spatial and circumstantial construction of the work's storyworld. Arguably, the currency of Stothard's illustrations on the British and French markets for illustrated editions of Defoe's novel was such that their origin as book-defined visualizations was still likely recalled by users of the plates. Indeed, the popularity of Crusoe images meant that they were part of a visual archive that capitalized on the recognizability of Crusoe in various scenes, including the figure's 'transmedia character template' (Thon, 2019, p. 184).

Stockdale had commissioned Stothard to produce sixteen designs: two vignettes, which appeared on the title pages, and a set of fourteen full-page plates depicting 'the principal scenes described in the narration'. The latter visualized scenes from both the first part of *Robinson Crusoe* (volume 1 of Stockdale's edition) and from *Farther Adventures* (volume 2), although the plates were unevenly distributed across the two volumes, the first boasting eight full-page plates and the second only four. The series opened with Crusoe taking his farewell from his parents and concluded at the end of the second volume with a scene of destruction, though the slaughter of the savages occurring at the same time was not represented. Stothard's second illustration introduces the protagonist 'clinging to a Rock' ('Subjects of the Plates'), the shipwreck interpreted as the providential consequence of leaving his paternal home and of his disobedience. The remaining six plates in volume 1, with one exception (plate 3, depicting Robinson on the raft laden with the goods that he has salvaged from the wreck), introduce subjects not illustrated before by Stothard. The artist had already supplied seven plate designs for James Harrison's 1781 *Novelist's Magazine* edition: they visualize snapshots from Crusoe's island existence, including work in his cave (plate 4), his discovery of the footprint (plate 5), the rescue of Friday and the shooting of a savage pursuing him (plate 6), the building of a boat by Crusoe and Man Friday (plate 7) and their construction of a tent to accommodate Friday's father and the Spaniard (plate 8). Crusoe is not represented as a reflective and inward-looking individual but as an active, secular force colonizing the island and establishing himself as its master. Plates 12 to 14 capture moments related to Crusoe once he has returned to his plantation in *Farther Adventures*. The frontispiece, plate 11, depicts the protagonist's 'first interview with the Spaniards on his second Landing' ('Subjects of the Plates') who treat him as 'a monarch, or a great conqueror' (Defoe, 1790, II, p. 42). Plates 12 and 13 focus on the English community on the island, the former introducing their 'Plantation', the latter rendering the flight of the Englishmen's families as savages land on the island with the intention of destroying the colonizers' habitations and slaughtering them. The final plate visualizes the burning of the Indians' boats by the Englishmen and Spaniards.

The illustrations for volume 2, in contrast to those for the first part of the novel, introduced scenes that, with the exception of the frontispiece, no longer featured Crusoe. In fact, the events chosen for iconic representation relate to him only: he did not participate in them. As a result, his presence, even in the frontispiece, is detached from the actions on which Stothard would concentrate in his subsequent designs. Crusoe's absence from three of the plates meant that one quarter of the Montereau plates did not introduce Defoe's hero to French viewers. Altogether, then, the four engravings in volume 2 do not engage with his adventures and concrete instances of infrastructure-building and resource management; rather, they capture episodes that occurred in his absence and that illuminate his colony's measures to ensure survival. In one illustration only, Crusoe's meeting with the Spaniards, the reunion between the protagonist and the Spanish 'governor' is rendered in visual terms strongly reminiscent of a religious leader meeting his disciples, the venerable Crusoe standing at the centre of the plate and flanked by the Spaniards who pay homage to him. At the same time, a different reunion, between Friday and his father, is taking place in the background. Understood within the context of the series as a whole, Crusoe's return to the island concludes his transformation from young and inexperienced man and colonizer to master and spiritual guide.

When Stothard's work was introduced in France, publishers sought to exploit his well-known reputation as an artist. The editor of the 1799–1800 Paris edition, Charles Panckoucke, an engraver, acknowledged on the title page that the edition featured Stothard's plates, '19 gravures d'après les dessins originaux'. Similar to Stockdale's work, it was a high-end edition, selling at prices of 18 to 22 francs (depending on its binding and the paper used), and for copies on *vélin* paper at prices of 30 to 34 francs.[35] Published by Panckoucke's widow, the edition, undertaken under the supervision of Claude Saugrain, was accompanied by full-page engravings accurately reproducing Stothard's designs. The plates also retailed separately and could be viewed, as the prospectus for the edition informed potential purchasers, as early as September 1797.[36] The visual apparatus of Panckoucke's volumes went beyond Stockdale's 1790 edition and was characterized as having been 'corrected by the ablest French artisans'[37]: it boasted three additional plates that Stothard had designed since the London edition's publication. Panckoucke's three-volume edition thus furnished purchasers with an amplified visual narrative.

That a French publisher reprinted English illustrations of *Robinson Crusoe* was not unusual,[38] but it is noteworthy that it was uncommon to credit the original source and artist of the plates. Stothard's plates enjoyed a unique position within the archive of illustrated editions of Defoe's novel: such was their popularity that between 1790 and 1908 they were reprinted at least twenty-four times in Britain and the USA; in addition, they were issued separately as furniture prints ('without the writing' and on India paper) at the time that Cadell and Davies published their 1820 edition, which featured a further augmented

---

[35] *La Clef du cabinet des souverains*, 17 April 1800, p. 8.

[36] *La Clef du cabinet des souverains*, 6 September 1797, p. 4.   [37] Ibid.

[38] The edition published by Seguin Frères in Avignon in 1809 reprinted, without acknowledgement of the English artists' names, the illustrations that had appeared in William Lane's London edition. J. McGowan & Son's undated edition had already reused the illustrations, and they were subsequently reprinted again in the 1812 Birmingham edition published by W. Suffield & Co.

visual apparatus, 'twenty-two Engravings ... from a Series of Designs by T. Stothard'. Furthermore, Stothard's designs were reprinted for the 1816 and 1821 Paris editions issued by Verdière. New engraving plates were produced for the 1821 volumes, the likely source of the designs for the Montereau plates, which therefore makes it possible to determine a production date for the faience plates after 1821. Verdière's later editions featured only twelve, rather than the nineteen illustrations of Panckoucke's edition. In the Preface to the 1821 edition, the editor insisted that once one has seen Crusoe on his island, one will remember it [this experience] for the rest of one's life ('une fois qu'on a vu Robinson dans son île, on s'en souvient toute sa vie' (Preface, 1821, p. vi)). The editor likens the reading of the work to a visual process in which the scenes described gain shape through imaginative concretization; in the context of the edition featuring Stothard's illustration, the reader's 'seeing' of the protagonist would necessarily be effected through the plates accompanying the novel.

This emphasis on 'seeing' Crusoe's adventures and doing so in as painterly a manner as possible had underpinned Stockdale's edition. At the time of their publication, the engraved illustrations represented the most comprehensive visualization of *Robinson Crusoe* in Britain. Stockdale's project, which sold at a substantial subscription price of 1 guinea, presented collectors with an unrivalled visual apparatus. The publisher stressed in his advertisements that 'the Plates alone are worth more than the Price of the whole Book', a reviewer noting that Defoe's 'well-known work appears in a dress suitable to its celebrity'.[39] The four pages of shorthand titles and quotations from Defoe's work also feature directions to the binder regarding the placement of the engravings, glossed as the 'Subjects of the Plates'. An 'instance of eighteenth-century narrative painting' (Blewett, 1995, pp. 48–9), Stothard's series marked a departure from earlier visualizations: 'de-emphasizing the solitary aspect of *Robinson Crusoe* and illustrating more social scenes', the artist shifts the narrative's 'import away from moral instruction ... increasing the reader's identification with Crusoe' while at the same time 'reconstructing the natural world in a more attractive and detailed manner' (Blewett, 1995, p. 50, p. 52; Lipski, 2019, p. 92).

Panckoucke issued his edition at a time when a diverse material culture related to *Robinson Crusoe* was being produced: from glazed Staffordshire figurines of Crusoe and Friday, spill vases incorporating visualizations of the two characters to relief-moulded plaques and toby jugs of the eponymous hero and paper theatres. In marked contrast to the set of Montereau plates, these objects were characterized by their singleness. They offered versions of Crusoe

---

[39] *Critical Review; or Annals of Literature*, 2 (1791), p. 480.

(and Friday) that signified on their own and did not require other medially related objects to generate a larger version of Defoe's narrative collectively and in reference to one another. Such distribution of a story and the construction of a storyworld of characters, actions and settings across a number of identical text-technologically enhanced media became possible and cost-effective through transfer-printing applied to objects that formed collectives and series such as sets of speaking plates. Their producers targeted the middle classes and manufactured these tablewares in numbers that promoted the speaking plate as not only a genre of literary material culture but also a signifier of democratized cultural education. The single plate's portability and detachability from the remaining parts of the Montereau set allowed a mobility that made possible its comprehension on its own terms, rather than exclusively in terms of its relational embeddedness as a part of a greater whole: 'Each plate makes sense both on its own and as part of the series.'[40] At the same time, each plate featured a different design of a scene from *Robinson Crusoe*: working together, these images of moments from the story generated a master narrative or multiple narratives, but interpreted according to the viewer's ordering of iconic informa-tion. The series functioned in different social contexts because 'Speaking plates were either ornamental or used for desserts. Some of the sets were collectors' items that took pride of place on dressers, mantelpieces or walls, while others were used for entertainment purposes, with the design gradually being revealed over the course of the meal' (*Speaking Plates*, p. 5). In each of these scenarios of apprehension, different storyworlds were imagined as one image was or several illustrations were contemplated.

On a much larger scale than in the eighteenth century, transfer-printing provided the means for the transmediation of literature onto ceramics from the second decade of the nineteenth century. Indeed, we now see entire series of engravings originally produced as book illustrations used on ceramic plates. In contrast to the literary material culture introduced in the previous sections, the production of a series departed from the singularity of an individual object mediating and, in the process, encompassing a literary work metonymically. A series of engraved illustrations represented a visual narrative that consisted of modally defined multiples that had been constructed to support and complement the telling of a story; once the engravings were bound in the edition of the work visualized, they followed a particular order. In Stockdale's edition, for example, the sequential experience of the plates as part of the reading process was anticipated by the list of subjects that preceded the specific text of *Robinson*

---

[40] *Speaking Plates. Printed Narrative Scenes on 19th Century Creamware. 10 February 2017– 21 January 2018* (Geneva: Ariana, un musée, Ville de Genève, 2017), p. 5.

Crusoe depicted. The glosses represent metatexts that determine meanings: they allow an understanding of the scenes realized, of course, but they also present an alternative version of the plates concentrated as a list of subjects, rather than distributed across the codex. Importantly, removed from the diachronic anchoring framework of the printed book, the illustrations infer narrative through their visualizations of scenes and moments: they are no longer sequentially arranged and physically fixed through the binding process according to the narrative that they previously accompanied. As a result, when transfer-printed onto plates, these illustrations do not offer contextual cues to identify a particular order in which they should be read. Instead, they rely on their beholder to establish an order in which to read the images.

Depending on the depth of familiarity with the work illustrated, the beholder (which includes viewers of different ages with varying degrees of visual and material literacy) may opt for a reading that differs from the authorial narrative. After all, breaking up Defoe's narrative into iconic moments that are, in the case of the plates, potentially separated from the set creates new versions of the narrative that are the result of missing vignettes or the misarrangement of the set into a series that does not follow the structural make-up of *Robinson Crusoe*. As a result of the fragmentation of the narrative and its distribution across media, a recuperative act of storytelling is invited that 'is all about piecing together, adding to, embellishing, editing, transforming, and translating' (Sundmark and Kérchy, 2020, p. 2). For the reader, 'piecing together' that which has been transmediated entails the making of connections between accessible, present parts (the illustrated plates) and absent text recollected or inferred.

In his work on literature and ceramics, Peter-Christian Wegner has demonstrated that faience, rather than expensive porcelain, played a significant role in familiarizing the middle classes with literary works. Writing about German and French contexts, he holds that the faience items featuring literary illustrations, which he characterizes as functioning as part of an explained decorative programme (Wegner, 2012, p. 11), appealed to the educational aspirations of the middle classes. Wegner records how manufacturers of faience in the French towns of Montereau and Choisy in the first half of the nineteenth century capitalized on the enduring currency of Defoe's work by copying book illustrations from editions of French translations of *Robinson Crusoe*. While transfer-printed faience had been available in France from 1808, the Montereau firm did not undertake its first series of twelve *Robinson Crusoe* plates transmediating Stothard's illustrations before 1821. The firm would reuse the artist's designs for a later series, the plates of that set being significantly larger than the earlier ones (Wegner, 2012, p. 90).

Stothard's illustrations, functioning as mnemonic-imaginative sites, possessed the power to help reader-viewers to recall the storyworld of *Robinson Crusoe*. Anna Bray observed that '[w]hoever has seen it never can forget the design of Crusoe bringing the things he saved from the ship to the shore on his raft, and the lovely and inviting sylvan scene in the background' (Bray, 1851, p. 120). In the same way that the image had imprinted itself on Bray's memory, children would likely remember a version of it from their early reading. For the illustration of Crusoe on the raft (captioned 'The Raft') was popularized among child readers through its reprinting in reverse, as a miniature woodcut, in John Golby Rusher's sixteen-page, half-penny Banbury chapbook edition. The six woodcuts that adorned Rusher's 32mo pages constituted a dominant iconic presence, transforming the chapbook as much into a picture book as a highly concentrated abridgement of Defoe's work (Figure 22). 'The Raft' captures the scene that in the typographical text constitutes only one sentence: 'I swam to the ship and satisfied my hunger with provisions, made a raft with spars of wood, and landed what provisions or goods were in the ship' (Defoe, undated, p. 6). The focus for the child reader falls on the raft and the 'provisions' salvaged, the central feature of Defoe's vignette, rather than on the background.

While Stothard's book illustrations in the 1799–1800 French edition had featured descriptive captions, these paratextual devices were not retained for the Montereau ceramics. Rather, new captions were devised. Those ones accompanying the engravings were shortened to be accommodated in the cartouches below Stothard's images on the plates (Figures 23 and 24). For

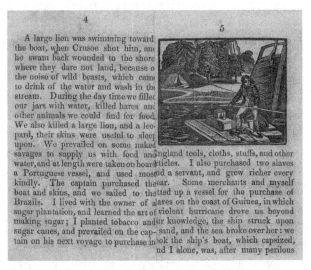

Figure 22 Woodcut '[The Raft]' (4.5 × 3.7 cm), *Life and Adventures of Robinson Crusoe* (Banbury: J. G. Rusher, undated). Collection Sandro Jung.

Pl. 3.

Je me rendois chaque jour à bord pendant la marée
basse; j'en rapportois tantôt une chose, tantôt une autre.
Tom. 1.ᵉ pag. 113.

Figure 23 Copper-engraved plate '[Robinson on the raft]', *La Vie et les Avantures de Robinson Crusoe* (Paris: La Veuve Panckoucke, 1800). Collection Sandro Jung.

instance, the illustration showing Crusoe on the raft was glossed on the Panckoucke engraving as 'Je me rendais chaque jour à bord pendant la marée basse; j'en rapportoix tantôt une chose, tantôt une autre'. On the Montereau plate, this gloss appeared as 'Robinson emporte du Vaisseau naufragé les objets qui lui sont nécessaires'. The gloss adapts the text of Panckoucke's edition but eliminates the statement regarding the regularity of Crusoe's expeditions to the wreck, focusing instead on defining the ship as wrecked and the objects the protagonist retrieves as necessary to his survival. The first-person perspective adopted for the caption in Panckoucke's edition is changed into a third-person perspective that necessitates Crusoe's introduction by name.

Whereas Stockdale had furnished a shorthand title for this plate in his list of subjects, 'Robinson Crusoe upon his Raft', it is the excerpt from the novel that follows this title that introduces the fact the protagonist had 'plundered the ship of what was portable'. The engraving in Stockdale's edition does not bear an

Figure 24 Transfer print on Montereau plate '[Robinson on the raft]', c. 1825
(diameter: 21.7 cm). Collection Sandro Jung.

explanatory caption. As a result, it does not direct the reading of the subject
depicted, including the relevance of the tent in the background as Crusoe's
temporary shelter, as it is denominated by the caption and cartouche text of
Panckoucke's edition and the Montereau plate respectively. It is likely that the
artisan responsible for the selection of cartouche titles for the Montereau series
derived titles from the reprinted illustration in Verdière's cheaper 1821 edition,
rather than from Panckoucke's. For Verdière, in addition to omitting Stothard's
name from the plate, also opted for simpler captions than those ones adopted by
Panckoucke. Verdière chose 'Robinson emportant diverses choses du vaisseau' to
characterize the design, a simpler version closely echoed by the Montereau plate
text. Stothard's original design, moreover, had introduced a detailed background
featuring trees, a large rock formation and Crusoe's tent. Blewett characterized
the scene as 'an idyllic landscape' (Blewett, 1995, p. 58) that had contributed to
idealizing Crusoe. In the design for the Montereau plate, no such idealization is
offered because these features are omitted altogether. Instead, the background
boasts a barren, mountainous landscape to underscore the necessity on Crusoe's
part to secure as many resources from the ship as possible to establish a more
permanent habitation than the tent that will provide him with a safe refuge.

　While the earliest French edition captions highlighted the personal application and labour necessary to manufacture objects ranging from furniture to
clothes that Crusoe finds indispensable, the cartouches of the plates reprinting
the illustrations for which these captions were first devised feature descriptions
that do not offer such qualifications. A gloss accompanying the book illustration

capturing the production of furniture emphasizes the effort it took Crusoe to turn carpenter, but it also notes that he manufactured only those pieces of furniture that he required most: 'Alors je m'appliquai à fabriquer les meubles qui m'étoient le plus nécessaires'. Again changing narrative perspective, the cartouche on the Montereau plate adopts the third-person, matter-of-fact statement that 'Robinson fabrique les Meubles qui lui sont nécessaires', the same as the caption in the Verdière edition, to concentrate merely on the action (Figures 25 and 26). Both the caption and the cartouche text, importantly, did not refer to the setting of this production activity, whereas it is centralized in the title provided in Stockdale's edition, 'Robinson Crusoe at work in his Cave'. To Stockdale, the interior of Crusoe's habitation represented a home that the protagonist had created through his own ingenuity. It introduced to reader-viewers the hero's family, the cats and dog, as well as an inventory of his tools. The version of Stothard's image included in illustrated editions differed in one important respect from the illustration realized on the well of the Montereau plate: it offered a view out of the cave on to Crusoe's fence, a large basket, a stool and an axe that are used as part of various activities to improve his habitation. Eliminating these iconic details from the design creates a scene without a background, the circular mouth of the cave replicating the circular

Figure 25 Copper engraved plate '[Robinson in the cave]', *La Vie et les Avantures de Robinson Crusoe* (Paris: La Veuve Panckoucke, 1800). Collection Sandro Jung.

Figure 26 Transfer print on Montereau plate '[Robinson in the cave]', c. 1825 (diameter: 21.9 cm). Collection Sandro Jung.

shape of the image on the plate, which, in turn, is prescribed by the shape of the well. Framed by thick black lines, Stothard's altered scenes are intimate glimpses into the storyworld of *Robinson Crusoe*. Similar to a telescopic view, they focus and enlarge the subject captured, but the new versions of Stothard designs also reduce detail that would have provided further cues for the imaginative expansion of scenes only evoked rather than fully represented.

The increasingly complex mechanisms involved in the transmediation of existing illustrations can be demonstrated by a later set of plates produced by the Creil-Montereau firm. The plates were produced between November 1849 and February 1854, the designs, signed by the engraver Pierre Lantz, allowing the dating of the plates (Bontillot, 2015, II, pp. 105–8).

The Creil-Montereau firm selected designs that have not hitherto been identified. Their identification has been made more difficult, since, in the process of adapting the illustrations for application on the Creil-Montereau plates, they underwent major compositional change. Notwithstanding the significant degree of alteration, there is no doubt that the plate designs were based on the wood-engraved drawings that the French caricaturist J. J. Grandville (a pseudonym for Jean Ignace Isidore Gérard) supplied for H. Fournier's 1840 Paris edition of *Robinson Crusoe*. Distinct from the earlier Montereau series, the Creil-Montereau set of plates offers viewers an ordering principle according to which to read the illustrations by numbering each plate. The selection of scenes that Grandville illustrated, as well as the changes in the figure design, reduced the caricature elements that the artist had introduced, a process that entailed the far-reaching revision of the earlier design of Crusoe discovering the footprint, and especially of his facial expression and gesture, for plate 8; the extensive adaptation of Grandville's designs also eliminated the 'ambiguity of the religious scenes' (Sitzia, 2020, p. 19, p. 13). The images at the centres of plates 2 ('Robinson passe sa première nuit dans un arbre') and 9 ('Robinson sauve la vie de Vendredi') are closest to Grandville's corresponding designs. In the case of plate 2, the general position of Crusoe sleeping in the tree has been retained, his crossed legs almost exactly copying the posture of Grandville's figure, although his arms have now been repositioned and his facial features appear younger than those of Grandville's Crusoe. Plate 9 offers a visualization of Crusoe's encounter with Friday (Figures 27 and 28). It does not render the by then paradigmatic image of the savage's submission to his saviour, the latter having just killed the cannibals. Instead, it introduces Friday as an individual who is fearful, shrinking from Crusoe's advance. In contrast to the changed version of the Grandville design for plate 2, that for plate 9 reverses the original composition and features an altered landscape, including a large tree in front of which Crusoe is standing. Whereas the transposition of Stothard's rectangular design frequently entailed a process of horizontal expansion or stretching to fill the entire area of the

Figure 27 J. J. Grandville, Wood-engraving '[Robinson encountering Friday]' (14.8 × 10.6 cm), *Aventures de Robinson Crusoe* (Paris: Fournier, 1840). Collection Sandro Jung.

Figure 28 Transfer print on Creil-Montereau plate '[Robinson encountering Friday]', c. 1850 (diameter: 22 cm). Collection Sandro Jung.

circular well, the illustration on plate 9 of the Creil-Montereau set compresses the composition on the horizontal plane: it positions Friday much more closely to Crusoe than Grandville had done, their feet almost touching. This reduction in the distance between Crusoe and Friday affects the way in which their relationship can be understood because even though he is fearful of his future master, Friday is physically close to him. This proximity suggests that their relationship will soon change, a change already signalled by Crusoe leaning on his rifle rather than holding it. He does not consider Friday a threat and invites his confidence with his hand gesture.

Grandville's designs of the scenes for plates 2 and 9 introduced Crusoe in the foreground. Their unframed, oval vignette format made them especially suitable for appropriation on the Creil-Montereau plates. When used on the plates, however, Grandville's designs, which frequently sought to create depth, have been changed to foreground Crusoe. The first plate in the Creil-Montereau series features a visualization of the shipwreck ('Naufrage de Robinson'), the protagonist having made it onto a rock, though the wreck of the ship is not visible. He faces the reader and, at the same time, confronts the hostile element from which he had just emerged. Grandville did not focus on Crusoe in the way that the circular image of the plate does. The French artist had rendered the survivor of the shipwreck with long hair, facing to the left, and he did not establish the direct rapport with the viewer that the artisan adapting the image for transfer-printing did. For use on the plate, Crusoe's facial features are rendered more expressively than they are in comparison with the less delicate realization of the face by Grandville. This lack of detail can be attributed, in part, to the representational possibilities and limitations of the wood-engraved medium: wood engravings are defined by a focus on line rather than by tonality. Grandville's image, though, is replete with detail, embedding his subject into a more complex seascape in which the wreck is visible in the far distance and the threatening weather conditions are more strikingly rendered. The Creil-Montereau plate, following the practice of the earlier Montereau series, opens the story of Robinson Crusoe with the shipwreck and Crusoe's arrival on the island. It does not feature any of the eighteen illustrations by Grandville that preceded the one on which the design for the first plate in the series is based.

The illustration adorning plate 3, captioned 'Robinson fait plusieurs voyages au navire', revisits Crusoe's salvaging goods from the ship: the wreck is seen only in the background, whereas the protagonist on his raft is approaching the foreground, the raft laden with chests, a barrel and tools (Figures 29 and 30). In Granville's design, Crusoe had not faced the viewer but was making his way to the wreck. In adapting the wood-engraved image for use on the plate, not only was the direction in which Crusoe is moving his raft changed but the stock of items he has saved has also been altered. In fact, the image on the plate merges two visualizations by Grandville consisting of the full-page vignette, captioned 'Je ramenai hereusement mon radeau et sa charge', and the smaller vignette preceding it that, closely copied in the illustration for the plate, offered a close-up view of the open chest and the barrel. Grandville's visualization of the raft scene had also boasted an individual in the far background, a detail that was not supported by Defoe's work, and this added detail was not included in the image for the Creil-Montereau plate, making it a more textually accurate rendering of the scene. Whereas the introduction of the figure in the background complicated an understanding of Crusoe as isolated individual, Grandville did not create a relationship between the two 'characters' central to the raft scene: Crusoe and the ship. These two entities are the foci of the Creil-Montereau plate, however.

The adjustment of details, perspective and position in the process of trans-mediating Grandville's visualizations does increase Crusoe's visible presence. His illustration of Crusoe's encounter with the turtles on the beach had presented reader-viewers with an overpopulated scene that not only included the large reptiles in the foreground but, departing from the text again, also added penguins. The Crusoe of Grandville's image stands in the background, carrying his rifle. He is accompanied by his dog, but he is far outnumbered by the animals

Figure 29 J. J. Grandville, Wood-engraving '[Robinson on the raft]' (13.3 × 11 cm), *Aventures de Robinson Crusoe* (Paris: Fournier, 1840). Collection Sandro Jung.

Figure 30 Transfer print on Creil-Montereau plate '[Robinson on the raft]', c. 1850 (diameter: 22 cm). Collection Sandro Jung.

depicted. By contrast, on the Creil-Montereau plate Crusoe has moved to the foreground and attentively observes the two turtles, a much-reduced version of the wood-engraved image that captures his surprise as he perceives the animals.

The scenes selected for the Creil-Montereau series repeated the subjects that Stothard had already illustrated and consolidated widely known vignettes of the novel's protagonist. But the transmediation of Grandville's designs involved an artisan who had to change the illustrations to make them suitable for the medium, eliminating inaccuracies and the visual conventions of caricature. After all, the purpose of the series of plates was to introduce Crusoe as a model of self-improvement and proactive agency, and this aim necessitated that perspectives and figure design be changed so as to create centralized scenes for the plates.

In terms of constructing the transmedial narrative, the numbered plates provided viewers with a chronology of Crusoe's adventures, which ranged from such scenes as his shipwreck and reaching land (plate 1), his recovering goods from the ship on his raft (plate 3), the building of his boat (plate 6), a scene depicting Crusoe and his family (plate 7), the discovery of the footprint (plate 8) and Friday's rescue (plate 9) to Friday's meeting with his father (plate 10) and Crusoe's departure from the island after more than twenty-eight years (plate 11). The numbering of the plates invoked an interconnectivity that relied on plate designs being apprehended sequentially, following the numerical order. In contrast to the earlier unnumbered Montereau plates, which could have been rearranged as part of the reading process, depending on connections being identified by the viewers, the later series was defined by a sequential order prescribed by the manufacturer. This order allowed less freedom in reading the plate designs in a way that departed from the numbered sequence, and gaps such as missing plates were immediately evident through the interruption of the numerical order.

In contrast to French producers of faience, who had adopted *Robinson Crusoe* as a subject for transfer-printing for a series of plates from the 1820s, English manufacturers from the 1840s started to produce Crusoe plates, especially for children's use. Compared to the twelve-plate sets manufactured in France, none of the English sets consisted of more than eight plates, each selling separately. In late 1847, moreover, the partnership of Bailey and Ball started to issue nursery ware that was embellished with transfer-printed designs based on Grandville's designs and usually, though not on all copies, featured short captions. The illustrative standard was uneven: some of the transfer-printed patterns were accurate reproductions of Grandville's designs, while others demonstrated significantly less care in the copying of figure design and details. The high degree of variation among plates reflects the large runs of plates produced by the firm. One feature common to all plates is the use of colour glazes, which enlivened the designs, even though the glazes were usually not carefully applied but dotted, at times even blurring the boundaries between different areas of the illustration by covering large parts of the plate well indiscriminately. Where visual revision of the original French designs was undertaken, it did not extend to rearranging the composition, as the Creil-Montereau artisan had done; rather, it entailed a process of simplification only, by which the tonality of the illustration and details not deemed necessary were reduced.

These early British nursery plates contrast with the more carefully coloured wares that the Brownhills Pottery Company started to manufacture in the 1860s (Henrywood, 2018, pp. 119–20). The Brownhills nursery wares included ABC plates and mugs, which featured transfer-printed, accurately rendered copies of the designs that John Gilbert had contributed to Thomas Nelson & Sons' 1860 London edition. Following the practice found on the Bailey and Ball plates, the captions added to the Brownhills wares were simple: 'Crusoe and his Pets', 'Crusoe at Work', 'Crusoe Finding the Foot Prints', 'Crusoe Making a Boat', 'Crusoe on the Raft', 'Crusoe Rescues Friday', 'Crusoe Teaching Friday' and 'Crusoe Viewing the Island'. These titles avoided the narrative positioning introduced in the captions of Stothard's full-page illustrations and Grandville's vignettes; instead, they provided concise representational glosses that helped child viewers to develop basic literacy by identifying the scene that they were viewing. The plates functioned as 'lesson-books' of sorts because 'simple lessons' were 'displayed on nursery plates and mugs'.[41] They served as literacy-enhancing tools with which children would engage, not only while eating from them but also beyond mealtimes.

Over a period of forty years, the application of scenes from *Robinson Crusoe* on ceramics changed significantly. In the 1820s, Stothard's sophisticated visualizations conveyed iconic knowledge of the work to the middle classes to whom the Montereau plates were marketed as desirable commodities. The Creil-Montereau firm's subsequent turn to more recent illustrations of *Robinson Crusoe* followed a veritable flood of illustrated editions and new representational styles that had appeared from the 1830s. The transmediation of Stothard's designs by the Montereau firm had involved a foregrounding of the protagonist within the circular shape of the transplanted image. Not only was the background removed from the artist's book illustrations, in the process eliminating visual contexts that were repeatedly genre defining, but this focusing on a central image also conveyed a sense of intimacy that the circular shape's visual similarity to a round vignette supported. The change in format from the portrait orientation of the rectangular engravings for Stockdale, Panckoucke and Verdière to the altered, circular image, but also the reduction

---

[41] *The Graphic*, 9 September 1893, p. 319. *South Wales Daily News*, 3 March 1899.

of tonality owing to the transfer-printing process and the elimination of depth, resulted in illustrations on the Montereau plates that were less specifically evocative. Specifically, their short captions reduced modal complexity, leaving it to the reader-viewer to reimagine both the situation visualized and how it cohered within the larger, recalled narrative of *Robinson Crusoe*.

The formal adaptation of Stothard's illustrations occurred largely because of the physical gestalt of the Montereau plates, which necessitated the change of format and spatial-visual revision. By contrast, the appropriation of Grandville's illustrations was more far-reaching, the major revision of the original wood-engraved designs producing transfer-printed images that were no longer faithful copies of Grandville's work. Rather, they were refocused vignettes that reordered the artist's well-known scenes in a manner that eliminated their ambiguity and caricature features. The processes at work in the transmediation of Grandville's designs went beyond the kind of iconic adaptation outlined in relation to *Pamela* and the tales from *The Seasons*. For, in merging several of the artist's vignettes, the artisan appropriating the vignettes for use on the Creil-Montereau set of plates reinvented the French artist's work. While Linda Hutcheon insists that adaptations represent 'inherently "palimpsestuous" works, haunted at all times by their adapted texts' (Hutcheon, 2012, p. 6), the transmediated Grandville illustrations on the Creil-Montereau plates escape any easy recognition because of the extent of their revision, even if their style is still strongly reminiscent of the artist's. At the same time, the palimpsestic nature of Stothard's illustrations was such that they would have been recognized, likely even highlighted, as deriving from high-cultural art by those people who sold and owned them. By contrast, the Creil-Montereau plates, in obscuring the iconic source of the illustrations in their wells, likely sought to highlight the novelty of these designs, as did Bailey and Ball.

The British manufacturer of nursery ware did not, as the French firm did, select illustrations that required visual revision but drew attention to image components through colour. In this case, the transmedial creation of meaning would work in particularly complicated ways. Since these plates retailed separately, they were not meant for relational reading, although connections could certainly be established if a child had access to more than one of the Bailey and Ball plates. Depending on a child's prior knowledge of the novel, the illustrations and captions functioned as self-contained semiotic systems that could be expanded through independent or supervised reading or oral instruction. These plate designs, and their captions, inspired interest in Defoe's work, opening up the work's storyworld for children. In this respect, the scene depicted on a plate could transform into a focus for engagement in which someone with textual knowledge could relate the text and image to one another for the child's benefit. The symbolic capital of the transmediated Grandville illustrations would not have mattered to children, though they would have imbibed those symbols, whereas it was the process of visual alteration necessitated by the transmedial migration from book to plate that signalled the Creil-Montereau's objective of promoting literary culture through fashionable visual art that was recognized as such.

6 Conclusion

As we have seen in the case studies, in the eighteenth century transmedially applied literary illustrations on material objects did not merely represent epitexts or textual echoes. They 'extended the experience of reading' (Williams, 2017, p. 153) and constituted the works that they remediate in a new form, but changed modally and amplified by the object substrates and text technologies that realize them physically. The process of transmediation re-occasioned existing illustrations. Accordingly, these materiality-imbued visualizations represent a synchronic moment that, while inferring both storyworlds and narratives, also recreates the stories of the objects that project and embody them. They are instances of 'literary visuality' and share a key part in literature's 'involvement in visual culture' (Isekenmeier and Bodola, 2017, p. 11); and they involve a process of medial migration that capitalizes on readers' ability to decode and synthesize literary, iconic and material meaning.

In a new history of literature that takes remediations of literary works seriously and incorporates them as part of a text's life and reception, illustrations should occupy a central place. Clearly, they provide valuable interpretive and metatextual commentary on the works iconically rendered. In contrast to book illustrations and separately issued prints, however, iconic objects featuring existing illustrations possess an esoteric particularity as material artefacts, including but not diminishing the multifarious performance of these objects in domestic settings. The transmedially used illustration functions as part of a decidedly more complex network of connections: it stands between typographical, inferred, recalled or reimagined text, image and object and illuminates the uniqueness of each object's social embeddedness. Because transmedially used illustrations frequently feature on elite artefacts, moreover, they transform an object iconically enhanced into not only an iteration of a literary work but also one that invites handling, tactility and desire. They function as imaginative sites, triggering viewers' recall through a process of reading and making sense of visual inscription. Absent from previous studies of illustrations and literary historiography, some of these objects, as well as their stories, have been rediscovered in this Element.

The case studies presented have charted, in particular, the mobility of illustrations, exploring how these visualizations rendered into a static representational gestalt a literary work involving characters, sentiment and action and signified as part of multi-medial iconic entities. The case studies suggest the various and complex ways in which literary meaning was advanced by illustrations once they were used on other non-literary edition media (mostly two-dimensionally but, on occasion, also three-dimensionally). Transmediation, because it involves processes of transformative adaptation and revaluation, removes the literary work represented from the codex and grafts it onto an object whose material-symbolic properties the illustration reinforces. As part of this process, its makers align the illustration – at times through revision – with the social practices governing the use of the object.

Remediations of texts represent instances of repetition, which in the eighteenth century was aided by practices of vignettization. According to Ann Rigney, it is 'the underlying portability [of stories] that enables them to move into different media and social contexts', which allows characters to become 'shorthand for a whole package of experiences and values' (Rigney, 2012, p. 12, p. 14). The visualization of these fictional individuals shaped, through the static capturing of situation, setting and action, interpretation of the specific image viewed in relation to Rigney's 'whole package of experiences and values'. The transmediation of literary illustrations on non-book objects invokes a special kind of non-identical repetition, however, because new medial relationships provide novel frameworks of reference for images defined by their literary-textual origin. Changes to the design, as in the case of the visual revision of Kauffman's and Hamilton's illustrations of Damon and Musidora (the resizing and refocusing of the illustrations, and the graphic redefinition of the lovers' connection in the design for the Duesbury vase) affect the readability of Damon's beloved. The vase's material-symbolic modality literally frames the altered visual meaning, as does the erotic modality of Birch's miniature. As Sarah Holloway notes, 'material objects do not exist entirely independently of texts' because 'objects acquired and conveyed meaning both through inscribed messages, their design, material properties' (Holloway, 2019, p. 71). Transplanting existing literary illustrations into material contexts for which they were not originally produced creates hybrid meanings, imbuing these objects with literariness at the same time as the repetition of these illustrations, including the subjects that they represent, are supposed to be recognized.

The sections of this Element have argued that the transmediation of the same illustrations forms part of a complex storytelling practice in which reader-viewers engaging with the iconically inscribed object identify, recover and reconstitute elements from the storyworld of a work. The versions of the storyworld 'read' and mentally generated not only are affected by the medial 'personalities' (Holloway, 2019, p. 70) of the objects featuring the illustration but they also register changes that artisans applied to designs to ensure specific interpretations. At the same time, the meanings of transmedially used illustrations could not remain static or stable – or even necessarily text-specific – because they are appropriated to visualize new subjects and stories and not simply to repeat the originals on which they were produced. The young woman depicted in Burney's illustration of Pamela and Mrs Jervis for an English edition, for example, is thus transformed into Fair Rosamond for a New York edition. Similarly, Francesco Bartolozzi's 1782 engraving of Angelica Kauffman's painting 'Shakespeare's Tomb' was adapted for use on a fan (the design being altered through the omission of the playwright's name from the memorial medallion) but functioned equally to commemorate Goethe's Werther and William Cowper respectively in young women's silk-work pictures.[42] These illustrations were pragmatically chosen not only because no cross-medial copyright governed their use but also because of their visual culture status as fashionable and sophisticated, non-typographical iterations of classic texts. Easily adapted to new occasions, novel frameworks of reference also reshaped their meanings, while potentially – as in the case of Kauffman's well-known design – importing (through recall of the image and any textual cues associated with it) Shakespeare's monumentalization to the appropriated design in embroidered pictures memorializing Werther and Cowper.

Manufacturers of literary objects were thus participants in a textual economy where adaptation and multiform media of literary expression played as important a part in cultural production as the promoting of their own interpretations of literary works to suit their clientele. Attuned to the commodity culture in which different iterations of the same texts and characters circulated simultaneously, and invested in the literary-symbolic-material literacy that helped them to understand illustrated and iconic literary objects as both material and narrative, consumers purchasing these objects will have been able to make sense of their literary-symbolic meanings. For the transmediation of illustrations constituted a widely used practice that conflated the symbolic capital of texts, images and objects. It was facilitated through technological innovation, specifically the use of reproduction techniques that made possible transfer-printing on a number of substrates, including ceramics. But it also stimulated the domestic, individualized (rather than commercial) production of needlework pictures.

Transmedially used illustrations on material culture produce resonance bodies of literary works. For beyond their text-derivative origin, they operated

---

[42] These adaptations replaced Shakespeare's name with that of Werther and Cowper.

within a complex feedback loop that qualified and affected how readers understood the work inferred: it worked well beyond a literal reading of the typographical text to engage with its iconic manifestation within a larger framework of material-symbolic meaning. These objects frequently functioned as display objects that were contemplated and discussed and that encouraged imaginative expansion or the over-layering of one narrative with another, as we saw in Lawrenson's rendering of Palemon and Lavinia as a sentimental vignette of Lady Sarah and the King's courtship. The transmedial adaptation of the artist's design on objects ranging from pitchers and mugs to figurines demonstrates how the same image could signify in different ways, especially where class politics were involved: indeed, changes in design indicated subtle rewritings of not only Thomson's vignette but also how the tale of the two lovers was mediated to different socially and nationally defined users.

The transnational use of existing designs on material culture was common, although studies of the Meissen manufacture's adoption of William Hogarth's 'Harlot's Progress' designs for use on a coffee set, similar to the numerous iterations of Wertheriana, remain to be undertaken. Whereas written cues to the meaning of the Palemon and Lavinia story had been limited to their names on the pitcher, the Montereau speaking plates reveal a more complex strategy to allow reader-viewers to understand the twelve individual scenes of the faience set. Detailed attention, on the paratextual level, was paid to the plate captions in the Panckoucke and Verdière editions and how, removed from the typographical text of Defoe's work, captions could function as part of a text–image unit on the plates. In contrast to the singleness of objects boasting transmedially applied illustrations, the series of plates conditioned new modes of apprehension. For narratives were distributed across multiple objects that, apart from the different design on each, appeared identical, an ordering principle supplied by the numbering of the plates or, in the absence of numbers, one generated associatively by the individuals viewing the plate scenes. The readability of the series, as much as of that of the Creil-Montereau set, was affected by visual alteration, the revision of the designs by Grandville significantly rewriting the illustrations' text-interpretive import. The gallery of scenes on dressers furnished viewers with a concatenated narrative in which connections were established through the spatial affinity of one plate to another or by the viewers' (mental) ordering of the scenes – or both. Viewing the present sequence of iconically inscribed plates overrides, in the interest of coherence, an accurate recovery of the absent (edition) texts, but in the process it generates potentially new meanings for a work.

The studies introduced in this Element have concerned themselves with the readability of illustrations as part of a mixed-media object that represents a version of a literary work. Transmediation generated objects that 'spoke', very much like the French speaking plates, to the purchasers and viewers of the vignettes studied. Invested in the material-textual-symbolic literacy of these artefacts, their beholders shared symbolic capital that included those literary characters who triggered stories through not only readings past but imaginative expansion. The stories, in turn, created a literary realm that both shaped and was shaped by those consuming these iconically enhanced objects, rather than being limited by the exclusive reading of the typographical texts of modern classics only.

References

Anonymous. (1783). *The Exhibition of the Royal Academy, MDCCLXXXIII*. London: The Royal Academy [*1783 Catalogue*].

Anonymous. (1796). *The History of Fair Rosamond, Mistress of Henry II, and Jane Shore, Concubine to Edward IV. Kings of England*. New York: J. Tiebout.

Anonymous. (1801). *The Exhibition of the Royal Academy, MDCCCI*. London: The Royal Academy [*1801 Catalogue*].

Anonymous. (1802). *The Exhibition of the Royal Academy, MDCCCII*. London: The Royal Academy [*1802 Catalogue*].

Bannet, E. T. (2011). *Transatlantic Stories and the History of Reading, 1720–1810: Migrant Fictions*. Cambridge: Cambridge University Press.

Barchas, J. (2003). *Graphic Design, Print Culture, and the Eighteenth-Century Novel*. Cambridge: Cambridge University Press.

Beattie, J. (1778). *Essays on the Nature and Immutability of Truth*, 2 vols. Dublin: C. Jenkin, vol. 2.

Bending, S. (2013). *Green Retreats: Women, Gardens, and Eighteenth-Century Culture*. Cambridge: Cambridge University Press.

Benjamin, S. (1999). *English Enamel Boxes: From the Eighteenth to the Twentieth Centuries*. London: Little, Brown.

Blewett, D. (1995). *The Illustration of Robinson Crusoe, 1719–1920*. Gerrards Cross: Colin Smythe.

Bolter, D. J. and R. Grusin (1999). *Remediation: Understanding New Media*. Cambridge, MA: MIT Press.

Bontillot, J. (2015). *Les Assiettes historiées de Creil & Montereau*, 5 vols. Sandillon: Les Amis de Faience fine.

Bray, A. (1851). *The Life of Thomas Stothard, R.A.* London: John Murray.

Bremer, T. (2020). Materiality and Literature: An Introduction. *Neohelicon*, 47:2, 349–56.

Brewer, D. A. (2005). *The Afterlife of Character, 1726–1825*. Philadelphia: University of Pennsylvania Press.

Brooks, A. (2010). A Not So Useless Beauty: Economy, Status, Function and Meaning in the Interpretation of Transfer-Printed Tablewares, in *Table Settings: The Material Culture and Social Context of Dining, AD 1700–1900*, ed. James Symonds. Oxford: Oxbow, pp. 154–62.

Chartier, R. (2007). *Inscription & Erasure: Literature and Written Culture from the Eleventh to the Eighteenth Century*. Philadelphia: University of Pennsylvania Press.

Cohen, R. (1964). *The Art of Discrimination: Thomson's 'The Seasons' and the Language of Criticism*. London: Routledge & Kegan Paul.

Colombo, A. (2014). Rewriting *Gulliver's Travels* under the Influence of J. J. Grandville's Illustrations. *Word & Image*, 30:4, 401–15.

De Bolla, P. (2004). *The Education of the Eye: Painting, Landscape, and Architecture in Eighteenth-Century Britain*. Stanford: Stanford University Press.

Defoe, D. (1790). *The Life and Strange Surprizing Adventures of Robinson Crusoe*. London: J. Stockdale.

(1799–1800). *La Vie et les Avantures de Robinson Crusoe*. Paris: La Veuve Panckoucke.

(1821). *La Vie et les Avantures de Robinson Crusoe*. Paris: Verdière.

(c. 1830). *The Life and Adventures of Robinson Crusoe*. Banbury: J. G. Rusher.

(1840). *Aventures de Robinson Crusoe*. Paris: Fournier.

D'Oench, E. (1999). *'Copper into Gold': Prints by John Raphael Smith, 1751–1812*. New Haven: Yale University Press.

Domingos, A. C. M. and J. A. R. Cardoso. (2021). Media Representation and Transmediation: Indexicality in Journalism Comics and Biography Comics, in *Beyond Media Borders. Volume 2: Intermedial Relations among Multimodal Media*, ed. L. Elleström. Cham: Palgrave, pp. 79–115.

Drakard, J. (1992). *Printed English Pottery: History and Humour in the Reign of George III, 1760–1820*. London: Jonathan Horne.

Dyer, S. and C. Wigston Smith, eds. (2020). *Material Literacy in Eighteenth-Century Britain: A Nation of Makers*. London and New York: Bloomsbury.

Elleström, L. (2019). The Modalities of Media: A Model for Understanding Intermedial Relations, in *Media Borders, Multimodality and Intermediality*, ed. L. Elleström. Cham: Palgrave, pp. 11–48.

Ferguson, P. F. (2018). 'Vase Madness': Vases and the Antique Taste in British Ceramics, 1765–1790. *English Ceramic Circle*, 29, 1–32.

Frankau, J. (1902). *Eighteenth-Century Artist and Engraver: John Raphael Smith*. London: Macmillan.

Genette, G. (1997). *Paratexts: Thresholds of Interpretation*, trans. J. E. Lewin. Cambridge: Cambridge University Press.

Girardin, R. (1783). *An Essay on Landscape; or, the Means of Improving the Country round our Habitations*. London: J. Dodsley.

Goldman, P. and S. Cooke, eds. (2012). *Reading Victorian Illustration, 1855–1875: Spoils of the Lumber Room*. Farnham: Ashgate.

Haywood, I., S. Matthews and M. L. Shannon, eds. (2019). *Romanticism and Illustration*. Cambridge: Cambridge University Press.

Henrywood, H. (2018). *The Transferware Recorder 4*. Bow, Devon: Reynardine Publishing.

Hodnett, E. (1982). *Image and Text: Studies in the Illustration of English Literature*. London: Scholar.

Holloway, S. (2019). *The Game of Love in Georgian England: Courtship, Emotions, and Material Culture*. Oxford: Oxford University Press.

Hutcheon, L., with S. O'Flynn (2012). *A Theory of Adaptation*. London: Routledge.

Ionescu, C., ed. (2011). *Book Illustration in the Long Eighteenth Century: Reconfiguring the Visual Periphery of the Text*. Newcastle: Cambridge Scholars.

Isekenmeier, G. and R. Bodola, eds. (2017). *Literary Visualities: Visual Descriptions, Readerly Visualizations, Textual Visibilities*. Berlin: Walter De Gruyter.

Jewitt, L. (1878). *The Ceramic Art of Great Britain*, 2 vols. London: Virtue & Co.

Jung, S. (2021). Isaiah Thomas's Illustrated Imprints in the 1790s: The Provenance, Uses, and Production of Their Illustrations. *PBSA*, 115:2, 137–66.

  (2020). Reinterpretation through Extra-Illustration: A Copy of Thomson's *The Seasons* at the Library Company of Philadelphia. *The Book Collector*, 68:2, 295–314.

  (2016a). The Other *Pamela*: Readership and the Illustrated Chapbook Abridgment. *Journal for Eighteenth-Century Studies*, 39:4, 513–31.

  (2016b). Thomson's *The Seasons*, Textual Mobility, and Bibliographical Inter-Iconicity. *ANQ*, 29:4, 220–9.

  (2015). *James Thomson's 'The Seasons', Print Culture, and Visual Interpretation, 1730–1842*. Bethlehem, PA: Lehigh University Press.

Keymer, T. and P. Sabor. (2005). *Pamela in the Marketplace: Literary Controversy and Print Culture in Eighteenth-Century Britain and Ireland*. Cambridge: Cambridge University Press.

Lipski, J. (2019). Picturing Crusoe's Island: Defoe, Rousseau, Stothard. *Porównania*, 25:2, 85–99.

Lopez Szwydky, L. (2020). *Transmedia Adaptation in the Nineteenth Century*. Columbus: Ohio State University Press.

Lucas, G. (2003). Reading Pottery: Literature and Transfer-Printed Pottery in the Early Nineteenth Century. *International Journal of Historical Archaeology*, 7:2, 127–43.

McGill, M. L. (2018). Format. *Early American Studies*, 16:4, 671–7.

McSherry Fowble, E. (1974). Without a Blush: The Movement Toward the Acceptance of the Nude as an Art Form in America, 1800–1825. *Winterthur Portfolio*, 9, 103–21.

Meyers, E. M., J. P. McKnight and L. M. Krabbenhoft. (2014). Remediating Tinker Bell: Exploring Childhood and Commodification through a

Century-Long Transmedia Narrative. *Jeunesse: Young People, Texts, Cultures*, 6:1, 95–118.

Mole, T. (2017). *What the Victorians Made of Romanticism: Material Artifacts, Cultural Practices and Reception History*. Princeton: Princeton University Press.

Montalvo, A. G. (2022). Novel Paintings: Learning to Read Art through Joseph Highmore's *Adventures of Pamela. Studies in Eighteenth-Century Culture*, 51, 23–48.

Müller-Scherf, A. (2009). *Wertherporzellan: Lotte und Werther auf Meißener Porzellan im Zeitalter der Empfindsamkeit*. Petersburg: Michael Imhof Verlag.

Napier, Sarah, ed. (1901). *The Life and Letters of Lady Sarah Lennox, 1745–1826*, 2 vols. London: John Murray.

Park, J. (2010). *The Self and It: Novel Objects in Eighteenth-Century England*. Stanford, CA: Stanford University Press.

Peterssen, S. (2020). Reframing the Concept of Illustration: Image, Text, and the Double Difference of Reproductive Media. *Konsthistorisk tidskrift/ Journal of Art History*, 89:4, 273–92.

Prown, J. D. (1982). Mind in Matter: An Introduction to Material Culture Theory and Method. *Winterthur Portfolio*, 17:1, 1–19.

Rabb, M. A. (2019). *Miniature and the English Imagination: Literature, Cognition, and Small-Scale Culture, 1650–1765*. Cambridge: Cambridge University Press.

Richardson, S. (2011). *Pamela, or, Virtue Rewarded*. Ed. A. J. Rivero. Cambridge: Cambridge University Press.

(1796). *The History of Pamela*. New York: J. Tiebout and E. O'Brien.

Rigney, A. (2012). *The Afterlives of Walter Scott: Memory on the Move*. Oxford: Oxford University Press.

Sanders, J. (2016). *Adaptation and Appropriation*. New York: Routledge.

Scarpaci, J. L. (2016). Material Culture and the Meanings of Objects. *Material Culture*, 48:1, 1–9.

Shepherd, L. (2010). *Clarissa's Painter: Portraiture, Illustration, and Representation in the Novels of Samuel Richardson*. Oxford: Oxford University Press.

Sitzia, E. (2020). Lost in Translation: J. J. Grandville's Illustrations of *Robinson Crusoe. Journal for Literary and Intermedial Crossings*, 5:2, 1–28.

Spencer, E. (2018). 'None but Abigails appeared in white Aprons': The Apron as an Elite Garment in Eighteenth-Century England. *Textile History*, 44:2, 164–90.

Straumann, B. (2015). Adaptation – Remediation – Transmediality, in *Handbook of Intermediality: Literature – Image – Sound – Music*, ed. Gabriele Rippl. Berlin and New York: De Gruyter, pp. 249–67.

Sundmark, B. and A. Kerchy, eds. (2020). *Translating and Transmediating Children's Literature*. Cham: Palgrave.

Taylor, D. F. (2018). *The Politics of Parody: A Literary History of Caricature, 1760–1830*. New Haven, CT: Yale University Press.

Taylor, G. (2009). In Media Res: From Jerome through Greg to Jerome (McGann). *Textual Cultures: Texts, Contexts, Interpretation*, 4:2, 88–101.

Thomas, J. (2017). *Nineteenth-Century Illustrations and the Digital: Studies in Word and Image*. Cham: Palgrave Macmillan.

Thomson, T. (1981). *The Seasons*. Ed. James Sambrook. Oxford: Oxford University Press.

(1777). *The Seasons. In Four Books*. Ed. G. Wright. London: J. French.

Thon, J.-N. (2019). Transmedia Characters: Theory and Analysis. *Frontiers of Narrative Studies*, 5:2, 176–99.

Treharne, E. and C. Willan (2020). *Text Technologies: A History*. Stanford: Stanford University Press.

Van Horn, J. (2017). *The Power of Objects in Eighteenth-Century British America*. Chapel Hill: The University of North Carolina Press.

Walsh, M. (2017). *The Portrait and the Book: Illustration & Literary Culture in Early America*. Iowa City: University of Iowa Press.

Warner, W. B. (1998). *Licensing Entertainment: The Elevation of Novel Reading in Britain, 1684–1730*. Berkeley, Los Angeles: University of California Press.

Watney, B. M. (1975). The Origins of Some Ceramic Designs. *Transactions of the English Ceramic Circle*, 9:3, 267–90.

(1972). Origins of Designs for English Ceramics of the Eighteenth Century. *The Burlington Magazine*, 114:837, 818–28.

Weems, M. L. (1800). *Hymen's Recruiting-Serjeant or, the New Matrimonial Tat-Too, for the Old Bachelors*. Philadelphia, PA: printed by H. Maxwell, for the author.

Wegner, P.-C. (2012). *Literatur auf Porzellan und Steingut*. Holzminden: Jörg Mitzkat.

Wigston Smith, C. (2013). *Women, Work and Clothes in the Eighteenth-Century Novel*. Cambridge: Cambridge University Press.

Williams, A. (2017). *The Social Life of Books: Reading Together in the Eighteenth-Century Home*. New Haven, CT, and London: Yale University Press.

Winterer, C. (2007). *The Mirror of Antiquity: American Women and the Classical Tradition, 1750–1900*. Ithaca and London: Cornell University Press.

Wolf, M. J. P. (2012). *Building Imaginary Worlds: The Theory and History of Subcreation*. New York: Routledge.

Acknowledgements

The preliminary work for this Element was undertaken as part of different projects on eighteenth-century British book illustration. I am especially grateful for the award of a Senior EURIAS fellowship at the University of Freiburg's Institute for Advanced Studies, where I was able to work on the transnational fortunes of *Robinson Crusoe*. Individuals who have shaped my engagement with book illustrations include Tim Erwin, Nathalie Ferrand, Ian Haywood, Stana Nenadic, Geoff Sill, Stuart Sillars, David Skilton and Michael Twyman. Others who constructively discussed my work with me include Jill Bepler, Carson Bergstrom, Gerry Carruthers, Michael Edson, Margaret Ezell, Daniel Fulda, Jim Green, Bernd Kortmann, Murdo Macdonald, Waltraud Maierhofer, Fiona McIntosh-Varjabédian, Jürgen Pieters, Cedric Reverand, Eleanor Shevlin and Kwinten Van De Walle. I am grateful to them all.

I gratefully acknowledge the support of the School of Foreign Studies at the Shanghai University of Finance and Economics and the College of Foreign Languages and Literatures at Fudan University, and I wish to express my indebtedness in particular to Xiaomei Qiao. In addition to my colleagues in the School, I am also beholden to audiences at conferences and seminars at Beihang University and Hangzhou Normal University where I was able to present earlier versions of the sections of the Element. Russell Palmer offered me the perspective of another discipline, which in this interdisciplinary undertaking was invaluable. The series editors of Eighteenth-Century Connections were enthusiastic about the project, as was Bethany Thomas at Cambridge University Press. Rebecca Bullard's early input proved useful, and Eve Tavor Bannet and Markman Ellis helped me to strengthen the Element and sharpen its argument.

Throughout the writing process, my mother provided me with scans and photographs of research materials, thereby allowing me the use of resources not available to me in Shanghai. She died shortly before the acceptance of the manuscript for publication, but without her contribution, this Element would not have materialized. I dedicate this Element to her memory.

Cambridge Elements ≡

Eighteenth-Century Connections

Series Editors

Eve Tavor Bannet
University of Oklahoma

Eve Tavor Bannet is George Lynn Cross Professor Emeritus, University of Oklahoma and editor of *Studies in Eighteenth-Century Culture*. Her monographs include *Empire of Letters: Letter Manuals and Transatlantic Correspondence 1688–1820* (Cambridge, 2005), *Transatlantic Stories and the History of Reading, 1720–1820* (Cambridge, 2011), and *Eighteenth-Century Manners of Reading: Print Culture and Popular Instruction in the Anglophone Atlantic World* (Cambridge, 2017). She is editor of *British and American Letter Manuals 1680–1810* (Pickering & Chatto, 2008), *Emma Corbett* (Broadview, 2011) and, with Susan Manning, *Transatlantic Literary Studies* (Cambridge, 2012).

Markman Ellis
Queen Mary University of London

Markman Ellis is Professor of Eighteenth-Century Studies at Queen Mary University of London. He is the author of *The Politics of Sensibility: Race, Gender and Commerce in the Sentimental Novel* (1996), *The History of Gothic Fiction* (2000), *The Coffee-House: a Cultural History* (2004), and *Empire of Tea* (co-authored, 2015). He edited *Eighteenth-Century Coffee-House Culture* (4 vols, 2006) and *Tea and the Tea-Table in Eighteenth-Century England* (4 vols 2010), and co-editor of *Discourses of Slavery and Abolition* (2004) and *Prostitution and Eighteenth-Century Culture: Sex, Commerce and Morality* (2012).

Advisory Board

About the Series

Exploring connections between verbal and visual texts and the people, networks, cultures and places that engendered and enjoyed them during the long Eighteenth Century, this innovative series also examines the period's uses of oral, written and visual media, and experiments with the digital platform to facilitate communication of original scholarship with both colleagues and students.

Cambridge Elements ≡

Eighteenth-Century Connections

Elements in the Series

A full series listing is available at: www.cambridge.org/EECC

Printed in the United States
by Baker & Taylor Publisher Services